# On the Sofa with
# Jane Austen

Maggie Lane

By the same author

# On the Sofa with Jane Austen

## Maggie Lane

THE CROWOOD PRESS

First published in 2016 by
Robert Hale, an imprint of
The Crowood Press Ltd,
Ramsbury, Marlborough
Wiltshire SN8 2HR

www.crowood.com

www.halebooks.com

**British Library Cataloguing-in-Publication Data**
A catalogue record for this book is available from the British
Library.

ISBN 978 0 7198 2058 8

Typeset by Catherine Williams, Knebworth

Printed and bound in India by Replika Press Pvt Ltd

# CONTENTS

| | | |
|---|---|---:|
| Preface | | 7 |
| List of Illustrations | | 9 |
| 1 | On the Sofa | 11 |
| 2 | The Hair was Curled | 17 |
| 3 | Lady Bertram's Fringe | 23 |
| 4 | A Very White World | 28 |
| 5 | The Silence of Mr Perry | 35 |
| 6 | Plump Cheeks and Thick Ankles | 41 |
| 7 | Reading Aloud | 47 |
| 8 | Arms and Legs Enough | 55 |
| 9 | November in the Novels | 63 |
| 10 | Words Overheard | 69 |
| 11 | Home Comforts | 75 |
| 12 | Shoelaces and Shawls | 81 |
| 13 | The Freshest Green | 87 |
| 14 | Neighbourhood Spies | 93 |
| 15 | She is Pretty Enough | 98 |
| 16 | Small World | 105 |
| 17 | Devoted Sisters | 111 |
| 18 | Theft and Punishment | 119 |
| 19 | Heroes and Husbands | 125 |
| 20 | Only a Grandmother | 131 |
| 21 | Dear Mary | 137 |
| Notes | | 141 |

# PREFACE

In a lifetime of thinking, talking, reading and writing about Jane Austen, I have found ever more to ponder and to admire in her novels. The essays in this book first appeared in the Regency World magazine as subjects occurred to me over the years.

In making my selection for this more permanent form, I have chosen those which celebrate the quirkiest corners and cleverest contrivances of Jane Austen's art. The title comes from the first essay, but it is also an invitation to spend time with a well-loved author in the comfort and intimacy of close quarters.

My special thanks are due to Professor Lorna Clark of the Burney Society, whose quest for an image so serendipitously sent me looking back through old issues of Regency World, and to Editor Tim Bullamore for giving my new project his blessing. On the Sofa with Jane Austen is dedicated to all my dear friends and colleagues in the Jane Austen Societies of the United Kingdom, the United States, Canada and Australia. I am particularly grateful for the support and interest of fellow writers Angela Barlow, Penelope Byrde, Susannah Fullerton and Hazel Jones, and for technical assistance to Hazel's husband David Brandreth.

Maggie Lane

# LIST OF ILLUSTRATIONS

| | | |
|---|---|---|
| 1 | Fanny Price on the sofa with Lady Bertram and Pug. | 8 |
| 2 | Mr Elton seats himself between Emma and Mrs Weston. | 10 |
| 3 | Willoughby takes a curl from Marianne. | 16 |
| 4 | Anne Elliot with her workbox in Bath. | 22 |
| 5 | Mr Perry on horseback. | 34 |
| 6 | 'Not handsome enough to tempt *me*.' | 40 |
| 7 | Mr Collins reads from Fordyce's Sermons. | 46 |
| 8 | George and Harriet Morland bring their news. | 54 |
| 9 | Dr Grant beckons Fanny into the Parsonage. | 62 |
| 10 | Nancy Steele eavesdropping. | 68 |
| 11 | Mrs Grant's sitting room. | 74 |
| 12 | Robert Martin busy with the umbrella. | 80 |
| 13 | Sitting under trees with Fanny. | 86 |
| 14 | Highbury gossips. | 92 |
| 15 | Anne encounters Mr Elliot at Lyme. | 104 |
| 16 | Jane and Elizabeth talking into the night. | 110 |
| 17 | Mary, Fanny and the necklace. | 118 |
| 18 | Edward Ferrars arriving at Barton Cottage. | 124 |
| 19 | Mrs Jennings shows off her new grandson. | 130 |
| 20 | A saucy smile. | 136 |

# 1

# ON THE SOFA

That fashionable article of eighteenth-century furniture, the sofa, appears in several of Jane Austen's most telling scenes. The word 'sofa' came into the English language with travellers returning from the East, where it denoted a raised platform strewn with rich carpets and cushions for sitting and lounging. In Europe, as increased leisure required greater comfort in the home, the name – sometimes spelt 'sopha' – was adopted for the elegant item of upholstered furniture that became an essential feature of genteel English drawing rooms. William Cowper, a favourite poet of both Jane Austen and *Sense and Sensibility*'s Marianne Dashwood, celebrated what he saw as a remarkable age of comfort with his long poem 'The Sofa', which forms part of his major work *The Task*.

In the poem the speaker marvels at the ingenuity of man for inventing such aids to luxury and ease as the sofa:

Thus first necessity invented stools
Convenience next suggested elbow chairs
And luxury the accomplished sofa last.

The speaker then takes a long and contemplative walk through the English countryside before returning for a well-earned rest on the sofa:

Nor sleep enjoyed by curate at his desk
Nor yet the dozings of the clerk are sweet
Compared with the repose the sofa yields.

The intriguing possibilities that distinguish the sofa from an ordinary chair for fictional purposes are, of course, the fact that it can be shared by two or more people; or, conversely, that it can be hogged by one person and used to put their feet up. Jane Austen exploits the possibilities of the sofa to illustrate idleness, illness (real or imaginary) and intimacy. Though most of her references to the sofa come in the novels of her later period, as early as her childhood writings she shows the sofa put to absurd use. For example, in 'Love and Freindship' the two heroines Laura and Sophia are described as 'fainting alternately on the sofa', while a two-year-old prodigy has the sofa to herself in 'Lesley Castle'. In *Pride and Prejudice*, dull-witted Mr Hurst, denied the game of cards he desires after dinner, has nothing to do but to 'stretch himself on one of the sofas and go to sleep'.

The personification of idleness is Lady Bertram, firmly anchored to her sofa throughout *Mansfield Park*:

> She was a woman who spent her days in sitting, nicely dressed, on a sofa, doing some long piece of needlework of little use and no beauty.

That she occupies a sofa rather than an ordinary chair suggests that she often has her feet up, leaning back at one end:

> Lady Bertram, sunk back in one corner of the sofa, the picture of health, wealth, ease, and tranquillity, was just falling into a gentle doze.

Only on two occasions does she apparently lower her feet to make room for somebody else. Once is when the child Fanny first arrives at Mansfield Park, and Lady Bertram invites her to sit on the sofa with herself and her pug; the only other instance is when Sir Thomas returns from Antigua and she becomes so unusually animated:

> as to put away her work, move pug from her side and give all her attention and the rest of her sofa to her husband.

Later, while the preparations for the ball go on all around her, Lady Bertram 'continued to sit on her sofa without any inconvenience', and she is still on the sofa during the ball itself, as:

> Mary, perceiving her on a sofa very near, turned round before she began to dance, to compliment her on Miss Price's looks.

The drawing room of a large country house would contain more than one sofa. Netherfield evidently has multiple sofas and so does Sotherton Court, where, on coming in from the garden, the young people 'lounge away' the time before dinner 'with sofas and chit-chat and *Quarterly Reviews*'. Lady Bertram's is not the only sofa in the Mansfield Park drawing room, though hers is usually its centre of attention. When Edmund and Julia walk in late one evening after dining at Mansfield Parsonage, they find Maria sullenly reading, Mrs Norris sewing, and Lady Bertram 'half-asleep', surely on her favourite sofa. Edmund wonders where Fanny can be, when:

> Her own gentle voice speaking from the other end of the room, which was a very long one, told them that she was on the sofa.

Presumably this is the long room in which the ball is later held, with the furniture pushed back against the walls.

Fanny's withdrawal from the family grouping, even for a few minutes, gives Mrs Norris a fine excuse to scold her:

> 'That is a very foolish trick, Fanny, to be idling away all the evening upon a sofa. Why cannot you come and sit here, and employ yourself as we do? … It is a shocking trick for a young person to be always lolling upon a sofa.'

Fanny rejoins the others immediately, while Julia does her the justice of protesting 'I must say, ma'am, that Fanny is as little upon the sofa as anybody in the house.'

Fanny is suffering from a headache, and most occupants of a sofa in Jane Austen's fiction are ill, or want others to suppose them so. In *Sense and Sensibility*, Marianne spends an evening 'lying weary and languid on a sofa' at Cleveland at the start of her serious illness. Marianne does subsequently take to her bed, but other invalids favour the sofa because it enables them to languish in full view of their families. In *Emma*, Mrs Churchill 'has not been able to leave the sofa for a week together' as Mr Weston informs Mrs Elton. And in *Sanditon*, Diana Parker writes to her brother from home that she is 'hardly able to crawl from my bed to the sofa'. When the three Parker siblings, hypochondriacs all, arrive in Sanditon and are visited by the heroine, Charlotte Heywood, that healthy young woman finds that though it is the evening of a fine summer day the window is firmly closed and the sofa placed as far from it as possible in front of a good fire.

Perhaps the most memorable case of an imaginary invalid taking possession of the sofa to obtain sympathy is Mary Musgrove of *Persuasion*, who is only twenty-three years old. Anne finds her 'lying on the faded sofa of the pretty little drawing room' of the cottage and complaining of neglect and feeling unwell:

A little further perseverance in patience and forced cheerfulness on Anne's side produced nearly a cure on Mary's. She could soon sit upright on the sofa, and began to hope she might be able to leave it by dinner-time. Then, forgetting to think of it, she was at the other end of the room, beautifying a nosegay; then, she ate her cold meat; and then she was well enough to propose a little walk.

The same sofa in Uppercross Cottage is the focal point of a little scene of equal pain and pleasure for Anne, when Captain Wentworth walks into the drawing room 'where were only herself and the little invalid Charles, who was lying on the sofa'. She longs to leave the room but is obliged to kneel down by the sofa and remain there to tend her patient. Charles Hayter walks in but only adds to the awkward atmosphere, and then:

> the younger boy, a remarkable stout, forward child, of two years old, having got the door opened for him by some one without, made his determined appearance among them, and went straight to the sofa to see what was going on, and put in his claim to anything good that might be giving away.

He climbs on Anne's back, will not heed her request to get off, and is silently removed by Captain Wentworth who, though not yet relenting towards Anne, cannot see her suffer without wishing to give her ease.

A little earlier in the novel, another sofa in another house – the Great House at Uppercross – is the scene of embarrassment for Anne. She has not yet got used to being in the same room as Captain Wentworth after an estrangement of eight years, when she finds that he is 'actually on the same sofa', separated from her only by the bulky form of Mrs Musgrove. Anne is effectively screened from Captain Wentworth, but she trembles because she can hardly believe that they are physically occupying the same sofa after all that has passed to estrange and divide them. She must learn to harden herself to such proximity, which she evidently experiences as a significant progression from simply being in the same room.

In an age of limited opportunities for physical contact, it is well understood that sharing a sofa with another of the opposite sex may be construed as a step towards intimacy, deliberate or accidental, welcome or unwelcome as the case may be. In *Emma*, when the ladies collect in the drawing room at Randalls after dinner on Christmas Eve, Emma and Mrs Weston are sitting on the sofa in comfortable womanly conversation when Mr Elton walks into the room. 'He joined them immediately, and, with scarcely an invitation, seated himself between them.' His intrusive bodily presence is bad enough, but he compounds the offence with his choice of conversational gambit. All that the polite Emma can do is to give him a look:

> but it was such a look as she thought must restore him to his senses, and then [she] left the sofa, removing to a seat by her sister, and giving her all her attention.

However, Emma finds that the trials of the evening are by no means over. She has to suffer the greater indignity of finding herself shut in with Mr Elton in the carriage going home, when he seizes her hand and professes his love. The sofa scene has nicely prefigured this, in showing Mr Elton as insinuating, unquashable and unable to read Emma's signals.

Emma Woodhouse is the only character in Jane Austen's fiction to *draw* a sofa. One of her sketches shows her baby nephew George snuggled down on the Hartfield sofa; her verdict on her own drawing is that 'the corner of the sofa is very good'. The valetudinarian Mr Woodhouse is never described as resting on the Hartfield sofa and, indeed, in Austen's fiction the use of sofas for repose is almost always associated with women; when men occupy a place on a sofa it is generally to stake a claim on the attention of a woman already sitting there. Even little Walter Musgrove is up to this masculine trick.

In November 1813, a month short of her thirty-eighth birthday, Jane joked to Cassandra:

> By the bye, as I must leave off being young, I find many Douceurs in being a sort of Chaperon for I am put on the sofa near the Fire and can drink as much wine as I like.

But it seems she rarely allowed herself the luxury of putting her feet up. Her niece remembered that during her last debilitating and long-drawn-out illness, she would not take the sofa for her own use, saying that her elderly mother would be prevented from lying down on it in that case and that she – Jane – was perfectly comfortable on three chairs pushed together. Perhaps, when she was really ill, she could not bear to class herself with the many characters whom she had shown seeking attention or idling their time away on a sofa.

# 2

# THE HAIR WAS CURLED

Whether as marriage-bait or status symbol, in Jane Austen's world a fashionable coiffure was highly desirable, though it cost some effort to achieve. When Emma Woodhouse at last gains the sanctuary of her own room after the trying journey home from the dinner party at Randalls and the anxious greetings of her family, there is another duty to submit to before she can be quite alone with her thoughts. 'The hair was curled and the maid sent away, and Emma sat down to think and be miserable,' begins Chapter 16 of *Emma*. Curling the hair by twisting it in papers before sleep made part of what Jane Austen herself in a letter called 'a world of torment as to hairdressing', though in her own case 'my short hair curls well enough to want no papering' while her long hair could be plaited up and bundled out of sight in one of the muslin caps she had recently made.

Virtually every mention of women's hair in Austen's fiction includes reference to curls. They were *de rigueur* for young women of the gentry class, signifying access to maids and hairdressers, time and leisure. TV and film adaptations of her novels have familiarized us with the hair fashions of the first two decades of the nineteenth century. The bulk of the hair would be swept on top of the head to be secured by bands or combs, with artful curls on the forehead, or short clusters of ringlets at the side or topknot, and tendrils at the neck.

Few were as fortunate as Jane Austen to have naturally curling hair. For most women, producing curls with only the aid of paper was hard work and had to be done every night, as we see with Emma. There was no direct heat, and no sort of setting lotion, even home-made. Jane Austen's friend Martha Lloyd's handwritten household book of recipes, remedies and beautifiers has nothing for the hair. The only application for hair given in the beauty manual *The Mirror of Graces* (1811) is this 'Wash for the Hair':

This is a cleanser and brightener of the head and hair, and should be applied in the morning. Beat up the whites of six eggs into a froth, and with that anoint the head close to the roots of the hair. Leave it to dry on; then wash the head and hair thoroughly with a mixture of rum and rose-water in equal quantities.[1]

Rather expensive commodities – and all this without running water and a shower-head. Naturally, it would require the help of a maid. An elaborate arrangement of the hair when going into company also called for help. In Bath, *Northanger Abbey's* Catherine Morland has her hair 'cut and dressed by the best hand' before her first appearance in public. Her hair is naturally 'lank', but her principal initiation into adulthood at the age of fifteen has been to curl her hair, a penance voluntarily undertaken for the sake of conformity and beauty.

Jane Austen speaks of getting help with hairdressing from various household maids over the years, though she never had the luxury of a lady's maid. In 1805 her wealthy sister-in-law Elizabeth paid a visiting hairdresser 5s (25p) for dressing her hair at home and the same amount for showing her own lady's maid how to do it. Jane herself, staying in the house at the same time, was charged only half that sum to have her hair cut, remarking wryly to Cassandra that Mr Hall 'certainly respects either our youth or our poverty'.

The same hairdresser attended a family party in London in September 1816 in preparation for a visit to the theatre. Jane wrote the next morning:

Mr Hall was very punctual yesterday & curled me out at a great rate. I thought it looked hideous, and longed for a snug cap instead, but my companions silenced me by their admiration. I had only a bit of velvet round my head. I did not catch cold, however.

Both Jane and Cassandra were thought by their nieces to have taken to wearing indoor caps to cover their hair – the garb of middle age – younger than necessary.

Going to a ball in Hampshire in 1800, Jane had no professional attention but 'my hair was at least tidy, which was all my ambition'. She makes occasional remarks on the coiffure of friends. Eliza Fowle (Martha Lloyd's sister) 'cuts her hair too short over her forehead', while a young lady of her acquaintance, visited at her fashionable school in London, 'looks very well & her hair is done up with an elegance to do credit to any Education'. Jane's wayward niece Anna, at the age of fifteen, had her hair cut short in an act of defiance. This was a challenge to the established norms of her class and gender. 'Anna will not be surprised that the cutting off of her hair is very much regretted by several of the party in this house

[Godmersham]' wrote Jane, adding philosophically, 'I am tolerably reconciled to it by considering that two or three years may restore it again.' Six months later Jane is still lamenting the effect on Anna's looks of 'that sad cropped head'.

The most famous woman of the period to crop her hair was Lady Caroline Lamb, another rebellious soul, though aristocratic enough to do as she pleased. The fashion did not catch on, and it was another hundred years before women in general discovered the liberation of having short hair.

With no direct description, most of what we glean from the novels about hairstyles comes from the remarks of other characters, or in some passing action. Thus, we can picture Marianne Dashwood of *Sense and Sensibility* as a girl of the 1790s because her curls are tumbled down her back when Willoughby cuts one off as a keepsake, as reported by her younger sister Margaret, who thinks this signifies an engagement between them. Elinor Dashwood, too, evidently wears her hair down her back, because when she sees a ring containing plaited hair on Edward Ferrars' finger, her immediate thought is that it must be her own, obtained by him without her knowledge, which would hardly be possible if her locks were all secured on top of her head. It was about the turn of the century when long loose curls became upswept to match the Grecian statue look of the Empire style of dress.

*Pride and Prejudice* too was first written in the 1790s, but though we know that Elizabeth Bennet has fine dark eyes, there is no clue to the colour or arrangement of her hair. It is mentioned only to illustrate her affection for her sister and carelessness of public opinion. This is when her hair appears 'so untidy, so blowsy' after her hasty walk cross-country to Netherfield, incurring the contempt of Mr Bingley's sisters who presumably would never be seen with a hair out of place – and who certainly enjoy the services of a lady's maid almost as elegant as themselves.

Ladies' maids were known by their surnames, all-purpose maids by their Christian names, like the homely Sarah who attends the Bennet girls at Longbourn. Towards the end of the novel when Mr Bingley arrives early for dinner, Mrs Bennet, her own hair 'half finished', runs into the girls' room in a panic, calling:

'Here, Sarah, come to Miss Bennet this moment, and help her on with her gown. Never mind Miss Lizzy's hair.'

In the same breath Mrs Bennet mentions Jane's sash, a true indication of the 1790s style of dress.

Two female characters in later Austen novels are as poor and socially insignificant as any she created, yet strangely perhaps seem to sport the newest fashion in hairstyles. Neither Fanny Price nor Jane Fairfax has a lady's maid to help her. Moreover, Fanny is extremely traditional and modest in all her ways. She is the last person to call attention to herself. We know she lacks the services of anyone except the upper housemaid to help her to dress – consequently, to do her hair – because of Lady Bertram's extraordinary action in sending her own maid, Chapman, to Fanny on the night of the ball – alas, too late to be of service. Her sailor brother William, his hand stretched towards Fanny's head, says:

> 'Do you know, I begin to like that queer fashion already, though when I first heard of such things being done in England I could not believe it, and when Mrs Brown, and the other women, at the Commissioner's at Gibraltar, appeared in the same trim, I thought they were mad; but Fanny can reconcile me to anything.'

What can he mean by this? It is as hard to believe a man would consider 'mad' – or even notice – a different arrangement of curls, as it is to believe in Fanny – and the colonial women – being 'crops', though something radical seems implied.

A few weeks later, that man of the world Henry Crawford describes Fanny complacently to his sister:

> 'her hair arranged as neatly as it always is, and one little curl falling forward as she wrote, which she now and then shook back.'

It is a mystery, only partially explained by William's having been out of England for seven years. The dating of *Mansfield Park* is uncertain (it was written in 1812–13), but only if William had left England in the 1790s – making the novel's action no later than 1805 – would he have seen a significant change in women's hair.

Jane Fairfax is more accustomed to the fashionable world and more consciously elegant, in her quiet way, than Fanny. In carefully attending to her own hair – which we know is dark, in contrast to her pale skin – even amid the privations of her grandmother's humble home she is maintaining standards, asserting her ladylike status, refusing to be defined by poverty. At the ball at The Crown, her doting aunt is diverted from complimenting Emma's own looks to enquire:

> 'How do you like Jane's hair? – You are a judge. – She did it all herself. Quite wonderful how she does her hair! – No hairdresser from London I think could.'

Earlier, at the Coles' dinner party, Emma catches Frank Churchill (another man of the world) staring across the room at Jane. He has to think quickly.

> 'I believe I have been very rude; but really, Miss Fairfax has done her hair in so odd a way – so very odd a way – that I cannot keep my eyes from her. I never saw anything so *outrée*! Those curls! This must be a fancy of her own. I see nobody else looking like her! I must go and ask her whether it is an Irish fashion. Shall I? – Yes I will.'

Of course, this is an excuse to go and talk to Jane, standing before her and placing himself in Emma's line of vision to obstruct her physical sight just as surely as he obstructs her understanding.

Frank famously travels to London to have his own hair cut, as a cover for ordering a piano for Jane. While female hairstyles are not mentioned in *Persuasion*, male hair becomes something of an obsession, reflecting the vanity of Sir Walter Elliot, of whom it is said that 'few women could have thought more of their personal appearance than he did'. Sir Walter would not be ashamed of being seen with Admiral Croft if only 'his own man' could have the arranging of the Admiral's hair. The poor Admiral cannot bear looking in mirrors. Sir Walter criticizes one otherwise handsome man for having sandy-coloured hair, and another, looking older than his forty years, for having 'nine grey hairs of a side, and nothing but a dab of powder at top'.

Jane Austen's own hair remained brown until her death at the age of forty-one. In accordance with the custom of the time, locks were cut off and made up into keepsakes – a ring or a brooch – for family and friends. It is pleasing to consider that what had occasionally been a torment to Jane herself became a consolation to those who had loved her so much. One such memento is on show at the museum in Chawton.

# 3

# LADY BERTRAM'S FRINGE

It is well known that 'work' is synonymous with 'needlework' in Jane Austen's novels. Sewing, both for utility and for decoration, was women's habitual occupation in the Regency period as it had been from time immemorial, and as it would be until the invention of the sewing machine.

It is easy for us to deplore the fact that women were expected to sew if they had nothing else to do, and to sympathize with lively heroines like Catherine Morland and Elizabeth Bennet for whom sewing is not a favourite occupation. Catherine puts aside her workbox with 'joyful haste' when there is another activity on offer, and when Elizabeth in a sudden fit of embarrassment wishes to hide her face from Darcy she bends over her 'work' with 'an eagerness it did not often command'.

Both these examples show that a woman was always to be found sewing in the daytime, whether she is away from home as Catherine is in Bath, or at home receiving callers as the Bennets are at Longbourn. Rarely do TV and film show this activity going on in the background, but this is an oversight: Jane Austen assumes her readers know that all her women seated indoors during the day are sewing unless she tells us otherwise. Usually she does not find it worth remarking upon, any more than she tells us every time her characters eat; but occasionally a detail emerges in the course of the story. In her London town house, Mrs John Dashwood sits alone with her carpet-work (tapestry) while her husband writes letters in another room. In the drawing room at Mansfield Parsonage, Mrs Grant is occupied with her fashionable tambour embroidery frame while Mary Crawford plays the harp for Edmund. During her visit to Hunsford Parsonage, Elizabeth Bennet and her hostess Charlotte Collins spend part of each morning sewing while they talk, as we know because when Lady Catherine drops by she looks into their 'work' and finds fault with it.

When at home in London, it is Mrs Jennings' pleasant custom to go out shopping or visiting friends each day. She is a wealthy widow with a comfortable home and she can do exactly as she chooses. Her chariot is regularly ordered for one o'clock. A late and substantial breakfast, which we are told is 'a favourite meal' with her, sets her up for the day. And how do she and her visitors the Dashwood sisters spend their time between breakfast and going out? We find them 'setting themselves ... round the common working table'. Mrs Jennings begins by 'measuring lengths of worsted for her rug'. It is to be inferred that Elinor and Marianne likewise have some 'work' to occupy them. It would seem that young ladies never travel without a sewing project in their luggage. Mrs Jennings herself takes her 'carpet-work' to continue when she goes to stay in the home of her daughter Charlotte.

For all its potential for tedium, from her letters we know that Jane Austen enjoyed needlework herself, and there were certainly positive aspects to this all-pervasive element of female life. A woman who wanted to be left alone with her own thoughts was greatly assisted by having something visible and useful to occupy her hands. And when engaged in collectively, needlework could serve as a bonding mechanism between women, facilitating easy, companionable chat. Add to that the sense of making a contribution to the clothing stock of the family or the local poor; and the pleasure of creating attractive articles for the person or home, when it was not easy to buy such things; and the satisfactions of female 'work' become more apparent. And it really *is* their 'work'. Women of the gentry class cannot earn money, but they can save it. For while husbands, fathers or brothers provide the income, women's skills were invaluable in making it go as far as possible, and in promoting the economy, comfort and status of the family.

This is why Austen deplores those women who do not take the trouble to learn to sew competently. She may agree with Darcy that 'netting a purse' is hardly one of the higher accomplishments, but she is scathing about slipshod or merely showy work. Into this category come the picture in coloured silks made by Charlotte Jennings at school, the footstool worked by young Julia Bertram which is too ill-done for the drawing room, and the yards of fringe made by her mother Lady Bertram, having neither use nor beauty. Certainly, Lady Bertram has to do *something* on her sofa all day long, but even with all this opportunity for practice, like a small child, she cannot help getting into knots. Fanny regularly has to get through the difficulties in her work for her, and on the only occasion that Fanny goes out for the evening without her aunt, among her preparations is to put Lady Bertram's work into such a state that she won't be missed.

When Sir Thomas returns after a two-year absence, Lady Bertram reflects that she has spent her time irreproachably: 'she had done a great deal of carpet-work and made many yards of fringe' though she has totally omitted to guard or guide her daughters' behaviour.

Fanny's own sewing is at the other end of the usefulness spectrum. She probably makes, mends and alters most of her own clothes, since the gift of a gown from her uncle on the occasion of her cousin's marriage is experienced as something really special. Her cousin Tom has certainly spotted that Fanny often has a needle in her hands, hence the innumerable workboxes, which are as far as his imagination stretches when he wants to make her a present. Fanny's 'work' is admired by Mary Crawford, who asks for the pattern and wishes she could work so well. One imagines that lively Mary has not much patience with sewing. On this occasion, she is kindly feigning an interest in her attempts to soothe Fanny's feelings after a spiteful outburst by Mrs Norris.

Fanny helps her aunt Norris with the green baize curtain and Mr Rushworth's satin cloak for the Mansfield theatricals, and undertakes her share – or probably more than her share – of sewing for the local poor. At Portsmouth her skills and her willingness really come into their own. Her young brother Sam is about to begin his career at sea, and their hopeless mother has not made all the clothes he needs for a long voyage. Mrs Price is no better at sewing than her sister Lady Bertram, with the difference that it really matters in the Price household – even their rug goes unmended. Fanny sees what is required and she sets about working for Sam immediately:

> and by working early and late, with perseverance and great despatch, did so much that the boy was shipped off at last with more than half his linen ready. She had great pleasure in feeling her usefulness, but could not conceive how they would have managed without her.

In both the letters and the novels, knitting is most often associated with the old and infirm. Old Mrs Bates in *Emma* is always to be found in the warmest corner of the little sitting room with some knitting in her hands, except when her spectacles break and leave her unable to work. A hard-working woman all her life, she does not like to be idle, though what she knits in an era innocent of jumpers and cardigans requires some thought. Mrs Austen, in her own old age, took up knitting gloves for all the family: 'at present she wants no other work,' Jane told Cassandra. We know, for example, that Jane Fairfax buys her gloves from Ford's, the haberdasher of the village. Though Jane Fairfax herself knits her grandmother a pair of garters, they, of course, would be hidden from view. It is probable that Mrs Bates, widow of a clergyman, knits for the poor, as does Mrs Smith of *Persuasion* on a smaller scale, having been taught the somewhat lower-status art of knitting by her nurse while bedridden. Knitted clothes were not really elegant enough for the gentry, but the poor could do with anything warm they could get.

Mrs Austen also knitted bedside rugs. Knitting and tapestry had the advantage that they did not require the same excellence of eyesight as fine embroidery, as they can be done to some extent by touch. Jane Fairfax marvels at her grandmother's eyesight after a lifetime spent on fine work. So much sewing went on in the daytime because artificial light was not good enough. Penelope Byrde, in her excellent book *Jane Austen Fashion*, cites the case of Mary Delany, whose botanical paper collages and embroideries were truly remarkable works of art that we can still marvel at today. But these required good light, and in the evening the busy woman had to take up a less demanding kind of work. 'At candlelight cross stitch and reading gather us together,' she wrote to a friend in 1757. 'My candlelight work is finishing a carpet in double cross stitch on very coarse canvas to go round my bed.'[2] Perhaps when Emma Woodhouse, in looking ahead to what her life might be like at 'forty or fifty' declares 'I shall take to carpet-work,' it is because she is aware that eyesight deteriorates with age.

Writing in the Victorian era proud of its inventions, Jane's nephew James Edward Austen-Leigh says in his *Memoir* of his aunt:

> Her needlework both plain and ornamental was excellent, and she might almost have put a sewing machine to shame. She was considered especially great in satin stitch. She spent much time in these occupations, and some of her merriest talk was over clothes which she and her companions were making, sometimes for themselves, sometimes for the poor.[3]

Several items in fine lawn fabric decorated by Jane in her famed satin stitch survive and are on show in the museum at Chawton, as is a patchwork quilt made as a collaborative effort by herself, her sister and mother.

From our post-feminist viewpoint it is easy to smile at Austen-Leigh's unconscious agenda. *Ladylike*: tick. *Contentedly domestic*: tick. *Charitable*: tick. But that does not negate the truth that Jane Austen did excel in needlework; also, that it seems to have been rather a pleasure than a chore to her; and that, within her circle of female relations and friends, she enjoyed the intimacy it fostered.

She did not, however, quite approve her mother's habit of darning stockings in full sight of visitors. Mrs Austen combined the social confidence of her aristocratic connections with the time-pressed business of a mother of eight, and she had no truck with what she saw as the misplaced shame of the next generation who would have only decorative sewing on display when visitors called.

Some of the more mundane work of making and mending was deputed to servants: Mrs Jennings recommends a maid who 'works very well with her needle' and Emma Woodhouse has the coachman's daughter Hannah come to the house to do needlework – almost certainly the plain needlework involved in keeping supplies of household linen in good order. Nevertheless, when every stitch that everyone wore had to be put in by hand, even in the wealthiest households much was undertaken by the gentry. While on a visit to her rich brother Edward's home, Jane told Cassandra: 'We are very busy making Edward's shirts, and I am proud to say that I am the neatest worker of the party'. She added, 'an artist cannot do anything slovenly'. Of course, she knew that while every woman of her acquaintance could sew, she only could write novels; but to her both arts were worthy of being practised at the very highest level she could attain.

# 4

# A VERY WHITE WORLD

Jane Austen was born into a severe winter – the month after her birth, January 1776, was notoriousty cold, and many of her childhood winters are on record as being exceptionally snowy across Britain. This was the tail-end of the so-called 'Little Ice Age' (climate change was ever with us), which was marked by the great Frost Fairs held on the frozen River Thames in London. During the seventeenth and eighteenth centuries there were 26 of these fairs in total, the last one being in January 1814, when it is said that an elephant was led across the ice to prove its safety. It was still snowing in March of that year, as Jane Austen herself attests. On the first day of that month Jane set off with her brother Henry from Chawton to London, making an overnight stop and arriving in the early afternoon of the following day. After unpacking, Jane wrote to Cassandra:

> It is snowing. We had some Snowstorms yesterday, & a smart frost at night, which gave us a hard road from Cobham to Kingston. Extra horses were put on to pull the coach.

Skating was a popular pastime whenever lakes or rivers froze. Although Jane Austen has no such scene in any of her novels, her brother Frank was an enthusiastic skater. In January 1807 she wrote from Southampton of:

> one of the pleasantest frosts I ever knew, so very quiet. I hope it will last some time longer for Frank's sake, who is quite anxious to get some skating; he tried yesterday, but it would not do.

A month later she reported 'two of the severest frosts since the winter began, preceded by rain, hail and snow.' This was the Austens' first winter in Southampton, and with Cassandra on a visit to Kent, Jane wrote to her:

> You must have had more snow at Godmersham than we had here. On Wednesday morning there was a thin covering of it over the fields and roofs of the houses, but I do not think there was any left the next day. Everybody used to Southampton says that Snow never lies more than 24 hours near it.

Snow and frost make their presence felt in several of Jane Austen's novels, all of which contain passages set in winter. In *Pride and Prejudice,* the Bennet sisters' walks to Meryton during the months of January and February are 'sometimes dirty and sometimes cold,' but no actual fall of snow impedes them. In *Sense and Sensibility,* the Dashwood sisters and Mrs Jennings manage the three-day journey from Devonshire to London in the first week of January without inconvenience from the weather. In fact, we are told that it is exceptionally mild for the time of year. Marianne, fretting to hear from Willoughby, is comforted by the thought that he may be lingering in the country to enjoy the last of the hunting while the ground remains unfrozen – 'open weather,' as Mrs Jennings calls it. 'But,' Marianne observes hopefully, 'frosts will soon set in, and in all probability, with severity. In another day or two perhaps; this extreme mildness can hardly last longer – nay, perhaps it may freeze tonight!'

For a while, Marianne remains 'happy in the mildness of the weather, and still happier in the expectation of a frost'. She is more attuned to signs of the weather to come than most of us are today, with our reliance on professional forecasts. She observes the direction of the wind, watches the variations of the sky, and imagines an alteration in the air. The high pressure and lack of cloud cover necessary for a freeze also manifest themselves in the way a domestic fire draws. For people who had only their own observations and experience to go on, every clue was useful. Marianne feeds her hopes by seeing 'every night in the brightness of the fire, and every morning in the appearance of the atmosphere, the certain symptoms of approaching frost', which she hopes will bring Willoughby to town. 'I can hardly keep my hands warm even in my muff,' she pronounces happily. 'It was not so yesterday, I think.' Her sister is alternately diverted and pained by these reflections.

In *Persuasion,* the only clue to seasonal weather is the 'roaring Christmas fire' at Uppercross, possibly also drawing well because of high pressure. Anne Elliot also journeys to a city – in her case, Bath – early in January. She travels in rain, however, and encounters no frost or snow during the following weeks, or at least, none that we are told about. Her sister Mary writes of 'dreadful weather' in February, but that probably implies rain rather than snow, making walking muddy, as writing from the country she envies the 'nice pavements' of Bath. But there *has* been a frost in Bath before Anne arrives. Her father tells her that:

> once, as he had stood in a shop in Bond Street, he had counted eighty-seven women go by, one after another, without there being a tolerable face among them. It had been a frosty morning, to be sure, a sharp frost, which hardly one woman in a thousand could stand the test of.

In *Mansfield Park,* set in the midland county of Northamptonshire, there is an extended snowy season shortly after Christmas. Edmund Bertram, William Price and Henry Crawford have all recently departed Mansfield, and Tom, Maria and Julia have long gone. Fanny enjoys the tranquillity and comfort of the reduced household at the Park, but for Mary at the Parsonage the loss of the three young men is felt keenly. With just her sister and brother-in-law for company:

> they were now a miserable trio, confined within doors by a series of rain and snow, with nothing to do and no variety to hope for.

After a week of this, and in desperation to hear something of Edmund, Mary:

> made her way to the Park, through difficulties of walking which she had deemed unconquerable a week before ... for the sake of at least hearing his name.

Having chatted to Fanny she returns in better spirits 'which might have defied almost another week of the same small party in the same bad weather', but the very same evening brings her brother back from London (he is evidently able to travel in snow), and shortly afterwards he makes his proposal for Fanny. When Sir Thomas visits Fanny in the poorly furnished upstairs East Room, which she has made her own, he is at first diverted from the very great news he has to tell her by immediately noticing that she has no fire: 'There was snow on the ground, and she was sitting in a shawl.' Mrs Norris has given orders that there should never be a fire in a room used only by Fanny, an order the displeased Sir Thomas countermands.

And so to the great snow sequence of *Emma.* First mention of its possibility comes when Emma is trying to find excuses for Mr Elton to cry off from the Christmas Eve dinner party at Randalls so that he can hang around Harriet, who is too ill to go. 'It is so cold, so very cold, and looks and feels so very like snow,' she says, that 'when you consider what demand of voice and what fatigues tomorrow will bring, I think it would be no more than common prudence to stay at home and take care of yourself tonight.' Mr Elton's passion for dining out being augmented now by his passion for Emma – which he imagines reciprocated – he declines to take the hint, and accepts a lift in Mr John Knightley's coach.

Meanwhile, Mr Woodhouse, too full of the wonder of his own going out in the evening and too well wrapped up to feel the cold, is less conscious of the weather than any of his companions.

> The cold, however, was severe; and by the time the second carriage was in motion, a few flakes of snow were finding their way down, and the sky had the appearance of being so overcharged as to want only a milder air to produce a very white world in a very short time.

Emma's two travelling companions present an amusing contrast. Mr John Knightley grumbles:

> 'Actually snowing at this moment! If we were obliged to go out on such an evening as this, by any call of duty or business, what a hardship we should deem it; and here are we, probably with rather thinner clothing than usual, setting forward voluntarily, without excuse, in defiance of the voice of nature, which tells man, in everything given to his view or his feelings, to stay at home himself, and keep all under shelter that he can.'

Mr Elton praises the use of sheepskin for travelling, and all the contrivances of a gentleman's carriage which shut out the cold. 'Christmas weather,' he observes cheerfully. 'I was snowed up at a friend's house once for a week. Nothing could be pleasanter.' John Knightley answers curtly, 'I cannot wish to be snowed up a week at Randalls.'

But that begins to seem a possibility when, after dinner, he goes out to examine the weather and informs the others 'of the ground being covered with snow, and of its still snowing fast, with a strong drifting wind'. The consternation of almost everyone is great. John Knightley rubs it in:

> 'Another hour or two's snow can hardly make the road impassable; and we are two carriages; if one is blown over in the bleak part of the common field there will be the other at hand. I dare say we shall all be safe at Hartfield by midnight.'

Sociable Mr Weston hopes the whole party will have to stay at Randalls, whereas his wife worries how she might allocate the only two spare rooms in the house. Not only is Mr Woodhouse terrified, but Isabella's alarm is equal to her father's:

> The horror of being blocked up at Randalls, while her children were at Hartfield, was full in her imagination; and fancying the road to be now just passable for adventurous people, but in a state that admitted no delay, she was eager to have it settled that her father and Emma should remain at Randalls, while she and her husband set forward instantly, through all the possible accumulations of drifted snow that might impede them.

'If we do come to anything very bad,' Isabella says, 'I can get out and walk. I am not at all afraid. I should not mind walking half the way. I could change my shoes, you know, the moment I got home,' to which her husband replies, 'Walk home! You are prettily shod for walking home, I dare say. It will be bad enough for the horses.'

George Knightley, instead of talking, has stepped out to make his own inspection, going as far as the Highbury Road, where the snow is nowhere above half an inch deep, with a few flakes still falling, but the clouds parting, suggesting that it will soon be over. He assures them that the whole party will be able to get home, either now or later. In a simple exchange between him and Emma (foreshadowing the sensible way they will settle their affairs when they are married) it is decided that the carriages should be rung for, as Mr Woodhouse will not be comfortable until they are all safely home. John Knightley naturally follows his wife into the first carriage:

> so that Emma found, on being escorted into the second carriage by Mr Elton, that the door was to be lawfully shut on them and that they were to have a tete-a-tete drive.

Jane Austen has brilliantly prepared for and contrived the proposal scene between Mr Elton and Emma, which ends with them both in a state of 'swelling resentment and mutually deep mortification'.

Emma rises the next morning to be cheered by 'the sight of a great deal of snow on the ground'. Though Christmas Day, she cannot go to church. Anxious to avoid meeting either Mr Elton or Harriet for as long as possible, she is glad that the next few days make it impossible to leave the house:

> the ground covered with snow, and the atmosphere in that unsettled state between frost and thaw which is, of all others, the most unfriendly for

exercise, every morning beginning in rain or snow, and every evening setting in to freeze.

Eventually the weather improves, all the characters resume motion, and Jane Austen's wonderfully realized snow sequence, having served its artistic purpose as well as giving us the incidents of real life, comes to its end.

# 5

# THE SILENCE OF MR PERRY

Jane Austen was approaching forty as she was writing *Emma*, which, though bearing the publication date of 1816, was in fact published a week after her fortieth birthday, in late December 1815. Turning forty is a milestone for anybody, but what better way to celebrate than with the publication – by the most prestigious publisher of the day – of your fourth book? Despite having every reason for optimism, and although she had not yet experienced any symptoms of the illness that was soon to beset her, as a thinking woman Jane could not but be conscious of the passage of years. 'I must leave off being young,' she had written ruefully to Cassandra in November 1813, two months before she began writing *Emma*. Her response to ageing was defiance and the continued celebration of youth and health. *Emma* was the first in a sequence of three novels – *Persuasion* and the unfinished *Sanditon* are the others – in which hypochondria and the manipulation of others through imaginary illnesses are derided.

After the physically weak and feeble Fanny Price of *Mansfield Park*, Austen created the complete opposite in her next heroine, Emma Woodhouse, who is 'the picture of grown-up health'. Emma has suffered from measles in her childhood, but otherwise hardly knows what a day's ill health is. Her fortitude of body, mind and spirit, her powers of recuperation after any emotional setback, not only make for an attractive heroine, but drive and dominate the plot.

The two 'love interests' – Mr Knightley (tall, firm and upright in figure) and Frank Churchill, the child of good fortune as Emma calls him – are equally robust. But many of the characters who surround these three suffer from ailments, real and imaginary. The village of Highbury has the reputation of being a healthy spot, but an array of minor illnesses adds to its credibility for readers. During the course of the novel we hear mention of sore throats, colds, flu, tuberculosis, biliousness, scarlet fever, measles, chilblains, toothache, headaches, palpitations, nervousness, rheumatism, gout and seizure (stroke or heart attack?). An old lady suffers the deafness and failing eyesight of old age while, at the other end of the life cycle, a baby alarms her mother by appearing not quite well. The narrative ranges from the perils of childbirth – 'Mrs Weston's friends were all made happy by her safety' – to the finality of death – 'The great Mrs Churchill was no more.' Suddenly in Austen's world, the fragility of the flesh is an issue.

To emphasize this concern with health, *Emma* is the only Austen novel in which an apothecary – Mr Perry – is an ever-present figure in the narrative, a professional man whose opinions are often quoted by other characters, though as readers we do not hear him speak. Jane Austen's own paternal grandfather, William Austen, had been an apothecary, and she knew that such men were regarded as tradesmen, or at best, if they spoke and behaved in conformity with the gentry's manners, as half-gentlemen; perhaps she did not have confidence in rendering their speech. Or perhaps she judged it more effective to keep Mr Perry and his advice tantalisingly in the background.

He seems to have plenty to occupy his time in administering to the community, who hold him in deep respect, none more so than Mr Woodhouse, who hangs on his every word. The gentlemen of the place refer to him as 'Perry', the ladies as 'Mr Perry', except for vulgar Mrs Elton who says 'Perry' just as she says 'Knightley', to Emma's disgust.

The name of Perry occurs over eighty times in the text of the novel. *Emma* is indeed replete with non-speaking parts: upper servants, minor professionals and tradespeople, all contributing to the vivid sense of a working community with which this novel breaks new ground. (And *Emma* is the *only* Austen novel in which a dentist appears – though he has to be consulted in London.) But none of these non-speaking characters equals the omnipresence of Mr Perry, or his frequent interaction with the gentry characters. When a group of them see him go by on horseback, they even speculate on whether he is about to set up with a carriage for his rounds, the inference being that he is becoming prosperous enough to do so. Frequent consultations with the richest man in town have undoubtedly boosted his income. But his neighbours and patients are not cynical, and seem pleased for him; they know how hard he works, out and about in all weathers. He is said to be bilious, but lacks time to minister to himself.

Emma is extraordinarily tolerant of the medical obsessions of her elderly father, perhaps because his fears encompass not just himself but all his acquaintance, and therefore seem less selfish. That Mr Woodhouse's valetudinarianism is to be treated in the comic mode is signalled in Chapter Two, when 'there was no rest for his benevolent nerves' until all the wedding cake has gone, and the chapter ends on a note of laughter as we see all the little Perrys with a slice of the cake in their hands, despite their father – obliged to humour his most lucrative patient – agreeing that such rich food might disagree with many people; and the comedy is intensified in the following chapter, as Mr Woodhouse earnestly tries to dissuade his guests from eating the good things that Emma, as hostess, has provided for them. In fact, in the course of the novel, though much is made of Mr Woodhouse's nerves and fears for himself and other people, he has no specific illness or disability to prevent his taking daily walks in his garden.

His daughter Isabella is rather different, because she claims to be never free from 'little nervous headaches and palpitations'. To readers it is all too clear these are induced by the nervous tension of living with a husband who rarely speaks to her with kindness and too often with barely concealed contempt. She may not put two and two together, but we can; and Emma herself is 'quick in feeling the little injuries to Isabella which Isabella never felt herself.' Isabella mollycoddles her children, being too apt to ply them with what Emma describes as 'false physic'. The whole family have been taken at some expense to the coast, sea air and bathing having been recommended by their doctor in town, Mr Wingfield (in whom Isabella has as much confidence as her father has in Mr Perry), 'for all the children, but particularly for the weakness in little Bella's throat'. Isabella's mind runs always on medical matters and she will never forget the kindness of Mr Weston in writing a note, 'at twelve o'clock at night, on purpose to assure me that there was no scarlet fever at Cobham', a place the family would have passed through on their return to London.

Colds are common. Jane Fairfax 'caught a bad cold' on 7 November and it is still 'hanging upon her' in February – though, of course, she has an ulterior motive in wishing to try her native air. At Christmas, Mr Woodhouse tells Isabella that 'Poor Mrs Bates had a bad cold about a month ago', and adds that:

> 'Perry says that colds have been very general, but not so heavy as he has very often known them in November. Perry does not call it altogether a sickly season.'

In London, however, as Isabella informs him:

> 'colds were never so prevalent as they have been this autumn. Mr Wingfield told me that he has never known them more general or heavy, except when it has been quite an influenza.'

This confirms Mr Woodhouse's opinion that no one can be healthy in London; and as for Bath, the only time he tried the waters, he claims, they nearly killed him.

The person with the worst winter cold in Highbury is Harriet Smith. Accompanied by feverishness and a bad sore throat, it is bad enough to keep her away from the Christmas festivities enjoyed by everybody else. A nice touch is Harriet's wanting to be nursed by Mrs Goddard – the most motherly figure in her life, and one whose kindness to the pupils in her care is proved by her dressing their chilblains herself. Emma is not afraid to sit at Harriet's bedside, though Mr Elton is afraid on her behalf:

> 'A sore throat! I hope not infectious. I hope not of a putrid infectious sort. Has Perry seen her? Indeed you should take care of yourself as well as of your friend. Let me entreat you to run no risks.'

It is perhaps strange that Isabella does not implore Emma not to visit Harriet and run the risk of bringing germs back to Hartfield. However that might be, Harriet's cold is an excellent plot device to keep her out of the way while Mr Elton makes his advances on Emma.

Harriet Smith is a healthy young woman and makes a full recovery. Jane Fairfax, also young, is more delicate in health, a reflection of her more delicate mind – rather like Fanny Price and Jane Austen's next heroine, Anne Elliot, whose emotional distresses are played out in their bodies. From the time of her entering into a secret engagement with Frank Churchill, Jane seems never quite well, and eventually the situation places so much stress on her that she falls victim to 'severe headaches and a nervous fever … her health seemed for a moment completely deranged – appetite quite gone.' Jane's mother had died of consumption (tuberculosis) when she was three, and there are fears that she has inherited the tendency. In the present crisis these fears intensify in her aunt and grandmother, though Mr Perry reportedly finds 'no absolutely alarming symptoms, nothing touching the pulmonary complaint which was the standing apprehension of the family.' There is little patient confidentiality in Highbury and everybody's health is freely discussed.

As Mr Perry seems to apprehend, Jane's loss of appetite can be seen as a reaction to her circumstances, confined to a small home with her talking, fussing aunt, and specifically to the loss of control in her life. Eating or refusing to eat is one of the few aspects of her life that she *can* choose for herself, immobilized and impoverished as she is, while her fiancé dashes about the country with perfect insouciance and even derives glee from the subterfuge they are obliged to practise. Jane's is a psychosomatic illness from which she recovers when a repentant Frank Churchill treats her properly and their engagement – renewed after she has broken it off – is brought into the open.

The chronic invalid in the novel is Mrs Churchill, who is suspected by Mr Weston and others of feigning or exaggerating symptoms to manipulate her husband and adopted son, Frank, into dancing attendance on her. But then – uniquely in the course of a Jane Austen narrative – she dies:

> A sudden seizure of a different nature from anything foreboded by her general state had carried her off after a short struggle … She had never been admitted before to be seriously ill. The event acquitted her of all the fancifulness, and all the selfishness of imaginary complaints.

The death is exhaustively discussed by the Highbury population (who have never met her) and they agree that she was probably in more pain than they had given her credit for, and that continual pain would try the temper.

At the other end of the social scale, Emma pays a charitable visit to a poor family stricken by sickness as well as poverty. With an inclusivity new to her work, Austen offers glimpses into the physical as well as the financial sufferings of the labouring classes of Highbury. Another case is that of old John Abdy. Clerk to the Reverend Mr Bates for twenty-seven years, he is now 'bedridden, and very poorly with the rheumatic gout in his joints.' Unable any longer to work, he must apply for parish relief to survive.

'Highbury was reckoned a particularly healthy spot', we read in connection with the popularity of Mrs Goddard's school yet, as we have seen, the characters suffer their fair share of illness. As background detail, their various, mainly minor ailments add convincingly to the portrayal of a community. They also have the effect of throwing Emma's own excellent health into relief. 'There is health not merely in her bloom, but in her air, her head, her glance,' as Mrs Weston says. Only once is Emma's health called into question, when she is at her lowest ebb emotionally, fearing she has lost Mr Knightley to Harriet. Mrs Weston, so perfectly attuned to Emma's looks, enquires whether she is quite well. 'Oh, perfectly. I am always well, you know,' she replies, and indeed her emotional turmoil is of very short duration, put an end to by Mr Knightley's unexpected proposal. Compared with that of all Jane Austen's other heroines, Emma's period of intense suffering is very brief – which is not to say that she does not have very many serious moments, when she confronts her own mistakes and resolves to be a better person. But Emma brings to her self-examination what Mrs Weston calls 'no feeble spirit', which carries her through all her difficulties. Coming between the sombreness of *Mansfield Park* and the wistfulness of *Persuasion*, *Emma* is that rare achievement, a profound novel in which health and happiness predominate.

# 6

# PLUMP CHEEKS AND THICK ANKLES

Like many novelists, Jane Austen often uses body size and shape as a reflection of character. When we meet Harriet Smith we are told that she is 'short, plump and fair, with a fine bloom, blue eyes, light hair, regular features and a look of great sweetness'. I think the reader immediately knows that Harriet is to be a lightweight character, and not just because of the shade of her hair. That word 'plump', though something rather to be admired at the time – plumpness signified good health and having sufficient to eat, and hence a certain social status – that word 'plump' is the one that tells us Harriet's tribulations are unlikely to be very serious. In literature if not in life, plumpness is incompatible with real suffering. As Austen herself points out, in a famous passage in *Persuasion*:

> Personal size and mental sorrow have certainly no necessary proportions. A large bulky figure has as good a right to be in deep affliction, as the most graceful set of limbs in the world. But, fair or not fair, there are unbecoming conjunctions, which reason will patronise in vain – which taste cannot tolerate – which ridicule will seize.

All Austen's heroines are slim, though it is not a word she uses. When we hear anything about the physical characteristics of the heroines, it is always in harmony with their mental qualities. Elizabeth Bennet is lighter and quicker on her feet than her sister Jane, just as she is mentally quicker and more agile. Emma Woodhouse's 'firm and upright figure' is the mirror of her mind, always firm in its opinions and always upright in its morality, however much she errs. Anne Elliot is 'an elegant little woman' with a 'slender form', which is suitable for one so self-denying and so much overlooked by her family. The difference between the Dashwood sisters is physically as well as emotionally depicted: Elinor Dashwood has 'a remarkably pretty figure' while Marianne's 'form, though not as correct as her sister's, in having the advantage of height, was more striking'. Her story will be more striking, too, and her behaviour less correct.

Two of Jane Austen's heroines appear first as unpromising children, and we see their bodies as well as their minds develop. Catherine Morland starts life with 'a thin awkward figure' and sallow complexion, though by the age of fifteen, 'her features were softened by plumpness and colour' and 'her figure' has 'more consequence'. She has pleasure in hearing her parents remark, 'Catherine grows quite a good-looking girl – she is *almost* pretty today'. Fanny Price's mother describes her at the age of ten as 'delicate and puny'. When she is introduced at Mansfield, she is contrasted with her girl cousins, respectively two and three years her senior, but so 'well-grown' that the difference in age seems much greater. Maria and Julia Bertram grow up to be 'tall, full-formed and fair' whereas Fanny, we understand, remains small, and glides lightly about when she dances. Nevertheless, during Sir Thomas's absence Fanny, now in her late teens, develops physically as well as mentally and, much to her embarrassment, her uncle notices this and remarks to Edmund about the improvement in her figure. Fanny hates to have her body looked at – which is why acting is anathema to her – yet Sir Thomas has been looking and assessing ever since she arrived at Mansfield, for Edmund says, 'Your uncle never did admire you till now – and now he does'. Edmund himself sees nothing wrong in this.

Henry Crawford, too, finds 'she must be grown two inches, at least' since the last time they met, six weeks before. Two inches in which direction? Costume historian Penelope Byrde believes that Fanny's first professionally made gown, the gift of her uncle, which she wears to the dinner party where Henry Crawford looks at her with new eyes, has been constructed to support the bosom, with underpinnings that Fanny's home-made clothes hitherto have lacked.[4] The complimentary remarks of Henry and Sir Thomas perhaps conceal the truth of what they are really admiring.

Men certainly do regard it as their right to look critically and to pass judgement on women's faces and figures. John Thorpe refuses to be seen driving one of his sisters because she has thick ankles. Sir Walter Elliot stands in a shop in Bath and counts eighty-seven women pass by without finding a tolerable face among them. He is forever remarking, in her absence, on the physical defects of Mrs Clay, which suggests that he is examining her minutely whenever he is in her company. He considers that the ageing face of Lady Russell does not bear examination by daylight, and refrains from calling on her in the clear light of morning.

General Tilney watches Catherine Morland in motion and praises the elasticity of her walk. Mr Darcy, having abused Elizabeth's looks at the Meryton assembly ('She is tolerable, but not handsome enough to tempt *me*'), at subsequent meetings 'detected with a critical eye more than one failure of perfect symmetry in her form'. He is evidently looking closely. Before long he revises his opinion and 'was forced to acknowledge her figure to be light and pleasing'.

At Netherfield to nurse her sick sister, Elizabeth becomes aware of Mr Darcy's constant gaze:

> She hardly knew how she could be an object of admiration to so great a man; and yet that he should look at her because he disliked her, was still more strange.

Darcy closes his book and looks up when Miss Bingley suggests to Elizabeth they take a turn about the room, and when invited by Miss Bingley to join them, he declines, saying that in walking this way they can have only two motives: either they have secret affairs to discuss (he knows they detest one another) or:

> 'you are conscious that your figures appear to the greatest advantage in walking – if the first, I should be completely in your way – and if the second, I can admire you much better as I sit by the fire.'

Miss Bingley, who craves any kind of notice from Darcy, pretends she finds the remark 'shocking' and 'abominable', while Elizabeth will not give him the satisfaction of any response. It is only when, with softened feelings, she encounters his portrait at Pemberley that she thoughtfully returns the gaze of the painted Mr Darcy, who is depicted with 'such a smile over the face, as she remembered to have sometimes seen, when he looked at her'.

Women grow plumper or thinner as their stories progress and their romances take a turn for the better or worse. Anne Elliot, who begins *Persuasion* 'faded and thin' through having endured many years of regret and sadness, famously has her 'bloom' restored by the sea breezes and stimulating experiences of Lyme. She attracts the admiration of a passing stranger, who turns out to be her cousin, a man who, like his namesake Sir Walter, sees nothing wrong in ogling women in public:

> Anne's face caught his eye, and he looked at her with a degree of earnest admiration, which she could not be insensible of.

On her return from Lyme, even the unimaginative Lady Russell finds Anne 'improved in plumpness and looks'; and when her father, who has formerly thought her 'haggard', next sees her, he pronounces her approvingly 'less thin in her person, in her cheeks'.

Isabella Thorpe is afraid she has 'grown wretchedly thin' with love for James Morland, though this is, of course, only a self-romanticizing boast. When Jane Fairfax returns to Highbury, Emma Woodhouse surveys every aspect of her appearance almost with male eyes, judging 'her figure particularly graceful; her size a most becoming medium, between fat and thin'. Months later, at the height of her distress, Jane's appetite deserts her and, when Frank arrives to attempt a reconciliation, he is shocked by her 'wan, sick looks'. Marianne Dashwood fares yet worse. *Her* self-inflicted illness results in the 'hollow eye', 'sickly skin' and 'pale hand' almost of a cadaver. Marianne and Jane Fairfax are alike in refusing food when under severe emotional duress. So, too, does Fanny Price when plunged into the squalor and anxiety of Portsmouth, causing Henry Crawford to observe that 'her face was less blooming than it ought to be'. These three young women all lose weight as a direct consequence of being trifled with by young men.

There is a rich strand running through English literature of fatness standing for good nature, ease and generosity, while thinness denotes a mean or devious character. 'Let me have men about me that are fat,' says Shakespeare's Julius Caesar, 'Yon Cassius hath a lean and hungry look'. Shakespeare's Sir John Falstaff is the archetypal jolly fat man. Jane Austen does not deal in stereotypes, but she sometimes finds it useful to draw on this tradition. In two of her elderly women, fatness is equated with good humour. *Sense and Sensibility*'s Mrs Jennings is 'a good-humoured, merry, fat, elderly woman,' while in *Persuasion* Mrs Musgrove is 'of a comfortable, substantial size, infinitely more fitted by nature to express good cheer and good humour, than tenderness and sentiment'. While Mrs Jennings is the more vulgar and voluble of the two, both are kind, generous and easy-going, but limited in intellect and perception.

At the other extreme is Mrs Ferrars, a mean-spirited, ill-natured woman who is described as 'a little, thin woman, upright, even to formality, in her figure, and serious, even to sourness, in her aspect'. A happy medium is Mrs Croft, 'neither tall nor fat,' possessing 'squareness, uprightness and vigour of form'. This slightly masculine look is a good match for the mind of Mrs Croft, who is as conversant with business as her husband, and takes an active direction in their affairs.

Among her real men, Jane Austen prizes uprightness of posture, a character-istic she gives to several of her older male characters, most notably Mr Knightley, whose figure shows to advantage amid the bulky forms and stooping shoulders of the middle-aged men of Highbury; and General Tilney, 'a very handsome man, of a commanding aspect, past the bloom but not past the vigour of life'. The General's military bearing remains with him into civilian life. Another 'fine military figure' is that of Colonel Wallis. We do not know his age but his acquaintance Sir Walter Elliot, aged fifty-four, can congratulate himself on having 'as good a figure' as the

Colonel, with whom he likes to see and be seen on the streets of Bath.

Pleasant, hospitable Mr Musgrove who, like his wife, is 'so very large' according to his daughter-in-law Mary, is Austen's nearest approach to the easy-going fat man of literary convention. Another jovial and hospitable character who we might expect to fall into that category, *Sense and Sensibility*'s Sir John Middleton, is actually described only as a good-looking man of about forty; his girth is never mentioned. An older man whose bulk denotes self-indulgence rather than good cheer is Dr Grant of *Mansfield Park*, 'a short-necked, apoplectic sort of fellow,' in Tom Bertram's phrase – a man whose death is actually brought on by eating too much: 'three great institutionary dinners in one week'. The female equivalent is *Persuasion*'s Lady Dalrymple, whose broad back, which seems rather unpleasant as Anne follows it into the concert room, is probably the consequence of too little self-restraint.

Austen's anti-heroes fall into two categories, the charmers – Wickham, Willoughby, *et al.*, who possess every grace of figure, and the repugnant, foolish bores, who are almost all overweight. Mr Collins is 'a tall, heavy looking young man of five and twenty', John Thorpe is 'a stout young man of middling height … and ungraceful form' and Mr Rushworth is 'a heavy young man'. Their minds are no more nimble than their bodies. The most extreme case is the greedy Arthur Parker in *Sanditon*, the novel that Austen left unfinished at her death. At the age of only twenty-one, he is 'heavy in eye as well as figure'. Meeting him for the first time, Charlotte Heywood is at least 'thankful for every inch of back and shoulders beyond her pre-conceived idea' in shielding her from the heat of his unnecessary fire.

Such young men offer no temptation to the heroines, though they sometimes complicate their lives. No overweight young man ever proves more worthy of a heroine's regard than his appearance suggests, but many an attractive man is found *less* worthy than he first appears. As Elizabeth Bennet says of Mr Darcy and Mr Wickham, about whose past she has just found out:

> There certainly was some great mismanagement in the education of those two young men. One has got all the goodness, and the other the appearance of it.

We know that many a man is led astray by his eyes to marry worthless females – Mr Bennet and Mr Palmer being cases in point, while Edward Ferrars and James Morland have narrow escapes. But young women, too, are liable to make errors of judgement when the correspondence between physical charms and moral virtue has been deliberately skewed by the author as a test for their powers of discernment – and just to add to the fun.

# 7

# READING ALOUD

'She read aloud with very great taste and effect,' Henry Austen tells us about his sister. 'Her own works, probably, were never heard to so much advantage as from her own mouth; for she partook largely in all the best gifts of the comic muse.'[5]

Oh for a recording of Jane reading *Pride and Prejudice* or *Emma*! We know that when she began writing, as a child, she did so partly to entertain her family, and we can picture her reading the comic fragments that we now call the Juvenilia to the occupants of Steventon Rectory, basking in their laughter and admiration. In the Chawton years of creative fulfilment, no doubt the women she shared a home with, especially Cassandra, often had the pleasure of hearing Jane read from her work. But the brothers were dispersed. Jane sent presentation copies of her novels on publication day to each in their various homes, and the way she records their 'Opinions' makes it clear they had not heard or read the later novels before publication. Maybe afterwards, when occasion arose, Jane could be persuaded to read to them. Or perhaps it was only Henry, deeply involved with her publishing career, who was so favoured. (Although even he knew nothing of *Persuasion* many months after it was completed.)

We know that he read *Mansfield Park,* in either manuscript or proof, as he and Jane travelled together to London in March 1814, two months before publication. 'We did not begin reading till Bentley Green,' she wrote to Cassandra, suggesting brother and sister took it in turns to read aloud to one another in the carriage. They got as far as the marriage of Maria Bertram – more than a third of the way through. How very entertaining the experience must have been for both of them! Once settled in Henry's house, however, they each took up their own book. Jane 'tore through,' as she puts it, the third volume of *The Heroine* by Eaton Stannard Barrett, while 'Henry is going on with Mansfield Park'. The next letter assures Cassandra, 'he likes my M.P. better & better – he is in the 3rd vol.'

One member of the family who, in reading aloud, fell short of partaking in the best gifts of the comic muse, to use Henry's characteristically pompous phraseology, was Mrs Austen. This is somewhat surprising given that she was an accomplished writer of comic verse, perhaps the best in the family. But we have Jane's word for this deficiency in her mother. Mrs Austen's own quick brain seems to have led to her reading at a too fast a pace. In January 1813, Jane's second novel, *Pride and Prejudice,* was published – anonymously, of course. Only Jane and her mother were at home in Chawton when the three volumes arrived, Cassandra being away on a visit. Shortly after, Jane wrote to her:

> I have got my own darling Child from London. Miss Benn dined with us on the very day of the Books coming, & in the even[in]g we set fairly at it & read half the 1st vol. to her – prefacing that having intelligence from Henry that such a work wd soon appear we had desired him to send it whenever it came out – & I believe it passed with her unsuspected. – She was amused, poor soul! *that* she cd not help you know, with two such people to lead the way; but she really does seem to admire Elizabeth.

Miss Benn, an impoverished spinster neighbour, was evidently invited – or begged to be allowed – to hear more of the book the next evening. Lucky, lucky Mary Benn! She had no idea of the significance of the occasion, of how privileged she was. (Nor of how her own name would be in print two hundred years later.) However, as Jane told Cassandra:

> our 2nd evening's reading to Miss Benn had not pleased me so well, but I believe something must be attributed to my Mother's too rapid way of getting on – & tho' she perfectly understands the Characters herself, she cannot speak as they ought.

It seems Miss Benn herself was not invited to take her share of the reading aloud – or, if she was, she declined it, in deference to her cleverer neighbours.

Reading aloud has the great advantage that everybody in the room is being amused, instructed or entertained simultaneously; no one is left out, everybody can contribute to any discussion arising from the book. With the acquisition of a new book being a relatively rare event, it spread the pleasure fairly among the company – though more often the passages being read would already be familiar ones – favourite poetry or prose. In poorer households the practice of reading aloud meant that only one candle was needed, the non-readers (provided they were not sewing) able to sit in a poor light but not get bored. (There is only one candle in the Portsmouth sitting room of Fanny Price's parents, which her father places between himself and his newspaper, without reference to anybody else's convenience.)

In the all-female household of Chawton Cottage, it obviously *had* to be women who read aloud, if anybody was to do so. But in the novels, it is usually men who read to women. The art of reading aloud was therefore not classed with female accomplishments like playing an instrument or singing. It was a gentleman's contribution to the entertainment of the evening, often undertaken to occupy the minds of women whose fingers were busy sewing – or, in the case of Emma Woodhouse, drawing. Annoyed by Mr Elton's fidgeting behind her while she sketches Harriet, it occurs to her to employ him in reading.

> 'If he would be so good as to read to them, it would be a kindness indeed! It would amuse away the difficulties of her part, and lessen the irksomeness of Miss Smith's.'
>
> Mr Elton was only too happy.

The sitting continues the next day, 'and Mr Elton, just as he ought, entreated for the permission of attending and reading to them again.'

Sewing might be the accompaniment to reading without Jane Austen saying so specifically, so commonplace was it for women to pick up their needle in every idle hour. When Henry Crawford and Edmund Bertram walk into the drawing room of Mansfield Park after dinner, they find Lady Bertram and Fanny 'sitting as intently and silently at work as if there were nothing else to care for', although, in fact, Fanny has been reading to her aunt from a volume of Shakespeare. Fanny, of course, is far too shy to read aloud to anybody but her uncritical, supine aunt, though it is surely to Lady Bertram's credit that Fanny 'often reads to me out of those books' – by which she means Shakespeare. When Henry picks up the volume and looks for the speech they had reached, Fanny does not help him: 'All her attention was for her work'. So it is very likely that the Bennet sisters and their mother are also sewing when their father invites Mr Collins to read to them in his first evening at Longbourn. Though Mr Collins readily agrees to assume the male role of reading to so many women – a fine opportunity for self-importance – he protests that he never reads novels and chooses instead Fordyce's *Sermons*, from which he gets through three pages with 'very monotonous solemnity' before Lydia can stand it no longer and interrupts him with some trivial communication to her sisters. Though her two elder sisters berate her for her rudeness, they are probably as relieved as she is when he takes offence and declines to go on.

And perhaps at Abbey Mill Farm, Mrs Martin, her daughters and their visitor Harriet Smith are sewing when, as Harriet reports of Robert Martin, 'sometimes of an evening, before we went to cards, he would read something aloud out of Elegant Extracts – very entertaining.' Though the Martins are a farming family looked down on by the snobbish Emma, this is just one proof among many that they have adopted the habits of the gentry and are rising socially through their own efforts at self-improvement. It is certainly interesting that it is Robert who does all the reading aloud – the young ladies do not take their turn.

It would seem that even *Northanger Abbey*'s Eleanor Tilney does not take turns with her brother Henry when they want to enjoy a new novel together. 'You undertook to read it aloud to me,' Eleanor remembers, recalling also that when she was called away for five minutes to answer a note 'you took the volume into the Hermitage-walk.' This was evidently not evening reading. Henry agrees:

> 'Here was I, in my eagerness to get on, refusing to wait even five minutes for my sister; breaking the promise I had made of reading it aloud, and keeping her in suspense at a most interesting part, by running away with the volume, which, you are to observe, was her own, particularly her own.'

The book in question is *The Mysteries of Udolpho* by Mrs Radcliffe. It takes Henry two days to read it to himself; it would have taken much longer to read aloud.

Though Sir Thomas Bertram is mentioned as reading to his family, there are no scenes in Jane Austen of the paterfamilias reading aloud at his own fireside, carefully excluding anything that 'would bring a blush to the young person's cheek'. Such a scene is more Victorian in character. Mostly, Jane Austen's readers-aloud are not the heads of their households but visitors, like Mr Collins and Mr Elton, who are invited to read by their hosts almost as a mark of courtesy. It gives them a chance to shine (or otherwise), just as the request to sing or play the piano does for a young lady.

One who disappoints at least some of his auditors is Edward Ferrars, staying at Norland, whose performance is criticized the next morning by Marianne:

> 'Oh! mama, how spiritless, how tame was Edward's manner in reading to us last night! … I could hardly keep my seat. To hear those beautiful lines which have frequently almost driven me wild, pronounced with such impenetrable calmness, such dreadful indifference!'

To which her mother replies, not unreasonably:

'He would certainly have done more justice to simple and elegant prose. I thought so at the time; but you *would* give him Cowper.'

Unlike Mr Collins, who rejects the young Bennets' choice of reading matter, the amenable and obliging Edward reads what others wish to hear, even when his powers are not suited to it.

The scoundrel Willoughby, who makes his appearance in· the Dashwoods' lives a little later, reads 'with all the sensibility and spirit which Edward had unfortunately wanted'. Like the drawing room at Mansfield Park, Barton Cottage – arguably Jane Austen's most cultivated household, despite its limited financial resources – has volumes of Shakespeare to hand. The Dashwood women are active in pursuing and enjoying the arts, and together with Willoughby have been reading *Hamlet* before his abrupt departure.

Willoughby resembles Henry Crawford (though the latter, being the creation of Jane Austen's maturity, is more subtly portrayed) in the combination of artistic sensibility with moral deficiency. Both read well – Crawford superlatively so. It is at Mansfield that the art of reading aloud is most fully discussed. As Crawford reads from *Henry VIII*, Fanny, despite herself, slackens in her needlework:

> she was forced to listen; his reading was capital, and her pleasure in good reading extreme.
>
> To good reading, however, she had long been used; her uncle read well – her cousins all – Edmund very well; but in Mr Crawford's reading there was a variety of excellence beyond what she had ever met with…. It was truly dramatic.

Even the indolent Lady Bertram adds her tribute, not surprising as the contrast to Fanny's gentle reading must have been great: 'It was really like being at a play'. Edmund avows that 'to read [Shakespeare] well aloud, is no everyday talent.'

Though it is clear from this passage that Fanny's female cousins, Maria and Julia, have been required to read aloud as part of their upbringing, its being chiefly a male preserve is acknowledged by Edmund and Henry as they:

> talked over the too common neglect of the qualification, the total inattention to it in the ordinary school-system for boys, the consequently natural – yet in some instances almost unnatural degree of ignorance and uncouthness of men, of sensible and well-informed men, when suddenly called to the necessity of reading aloud.

The art of reading aloud, they agree, consists of 'management of the voice, of proper modulation and emphasis, of foresight and judgement'. It is clear that Jane Austen herself has given considerable thought to what makes a good reader – and that consequently, as Henry Austen vouchsafes to us, she was a good reader herself. In this, as in other respects, was Henry Austen a model for Henry Crawford? It is not unreasonable to suggest that Henry Austen was able to judge Jane's performance because his own practice was as good, and his understanding as developed, as his namesake's.

# 8

# ARMS AND LEGS ENOUGH

'A family of ten children will always be called a fine family, where there are heads and arms and legs enough for the number,' the narrator coolly remarks in the first paragraph of *Northanger Abbey*. This is symptomatic of a generally detached view of children on the author's part, though she seems to warm to them and understand them better as she grows older herself. Jane Austen came to enjoy being an aunt very much and to delight in the individuality of her various nephews and nieces, though never blinded by affection into losing her critical faculties.

Charming or spoilt, children in Jane Austen's novels do more than just contribute to a realistic picture of family life. When contemplating her fictional children, those in *Sense and Sensibility* are apt to spring first to mind. Who could forget the spoilt brats of Sir John and Lady Middleton, whose role is to point up the doting nature of their empty-minded mother and the obnoxious flattery of visitors Nancy and Lucy Steele. 'I love to see children full of life and spirits; I cannot bear them if they are tame and quiet,' claims Lucy, to which Elinor replies drily, 'while I am at Barton Park, I never think of tame and quiet children with any abhorrence.'

Hardly less indulged is the same novel's Harry Dashwood who, despite his tender years, has been the means of depriving the heroines of the fortune that should be theirs. Instead of leaving his estate unencumbered to their father, old Mr Dashwood secures it to their half-brother and his son, having been won over 'by such attractions as are by no means unusual in children of two or three years old: an imperfect articulation, an earnest desire of having his own way, many cunning tricks, and a great deal of noise.' And when in fulfilment of a promise to his dying father, John Dashwood proposes to give his half-sisters a thousand pounds apiece, his wife demands: 'How could he answer it to himself to rob his child, and his only child too, of so large a sum?' She reinforces her argument later in the conversation by referring to the child as 'our poor little boy', though there is nothing poor about Harry. Personally innocent he may be, but as with so many of the characters in *Sense and Sensibility*, this child can hardly fail to induce dislike in the reader.

Jane Austen's harshness towards children in this novel extends even to poor Margaret Dashwood, who at the age of thirteen is dismissed in an early paragraph as having imbibed Marianne's romance without having her sense, and not bidding fair to equal her sisters at a more advanced period of life. It seems her potential is closed down before she has even begun to learn lessons from life. Elinor, such a good sister to Marianne, makes no attempts to guide Margaret and seems to have no tenderness for her; like the author, she appears to have written her off. Margaret is useful to the plot in keeping her mother in Devon while the two older girls travel to London, and in occasionally revealing secrets that her sisters would prefer to remain hidden, but there is so much more that her character, viewed in artistic terms, could achieve. The 1995 Emma Thompson film of *Sense and Sensibility* is, in my view, superior to the novel in that respect, showing a tomboyish charm in Margaret that must be suppressed in order to make her into an acceptable young lady according to the constraints of the period, meanwhile bringing out the playful best in Edward Ferrars (as played by Hugh Grant).

Having shaken off her apparent animus against children in *Sense and Sensibility*, Austen presents them as much more delightful in *Pride and Prejudice*, where they appear in the guise of the little Gardiners, first shyly on the staircase of their London home when Elizabeth arrives, and later at Longbourn, where they have been deposited in the care of their cousin Jane while their parents and Elizabeth travel to Derbyshire. It is clear that these children – two girls of eight and six, and two younger boys – have not been spoiled, and Jane's 'steady sense and sweetness of temper exactly adapted her for attending to them in every way – teaching them, playing with them, and loving them'. (It is disconcerting to find Mr and Mrs Gardiner, caring and affectionate parents, leaving their children in London when they visit Longbourn at Christmas; or at least it would be, were it not more likely to be an oversight on the author's part than neglect on the Gardiners'.)

The return of Elizabeth, her uncle and aunt from their Derbyshire tour is hastened and distressed by the news of Lydia's disappearance. As they arrive:

> the little Gardiners, attracted by the sight of a chaise, were standing on the steps of the house, as they entered the paddock; and when the carriage drove up to the door, the joyful surprise that lighted up their faces, and displayed

itself over their whole bodies, in a variety of capers and frisks, was the first pleasing earnest of their welcome. Elizabeth jumped out; and, after giving each of them an hasty kiss, hurried into the vestibule....

The experience of Jane Austen as the aunt of a growing tribe of nephews and nieces is detectable in this very realistic description. A similar scene takes place at the end of *Northanger Abbey*. Again, the setting is in the country, where carriages are infrequently seen, and again, the heroine is arriving home in some distress, which the naive delight of innocent children puts into perspective:

The chaise of a traveller being a rare sight in Fullerton, the whole family were immediately at the window; and to have it stop at the sweep-gate was a pleasure to brighten every eye and occupy every fancy – a pleasure quite unlooked for by all but the two youngest children, a boy and girl of six and four years old, who expected a brother or sister in every carriage. Happy the glance that first distinguished Catherine! Happy the voice that proclaimed the discovery! But whether such happiness were the lawful property of George or Harriet could never be exactly understood.

This touch of competitiveness is wonderfully observed.

In the abandoned middle-period fragment known to us as *The Watsons*, Austen offers a touching yet unsentimental cameo portrait of a child. Charles Blake, ten years old, is introduced into the plot at a public ball, where the young lady of the neighbouring Castle has promised to dance with him. When she goes back on her promise, preferring an officer as a partner, he is mortified. Emma Watson, to whom he is a stranger, 'did not think or reflect – she felt and acted' and offers herself as his partner for the dance, transforming his attempts at 'boyish bravery' in his disappointment to unfeigned delight in his pretty new partner. He is told by his mother to be sure to keep his gloves on – a nice touch. Emma finds the boy, 'though chiefly bent on dancing, not unwilling to speak', and when his shyness is fully dissipated, he tells her with boyish enthusiasm of what chiefly interests him at the Castle:

'There is a monstrous stuffed fox there, and a badger – anybody would think they were alive. It is a pity you should not see them.'

He is astonished to find on enquiry that it is eleven o'clock, as his mother had told him he'd be sleepy by ten.

This charming vignette was followed by something wholly new and rather ambitious in Austen's fiction: the portrayal of the heroine herself as a child. In the portrait of Fanny Price as a deeply feeling ten-year-old, Austen even anticipates the favourite plots of Charlotte Brontë and Charles Dickens. (Brontë had not read *Mansfield Park* when she made her attack on the elegant cold-heartedness of Austen's novels, or she surely would have modified her view.) Most of the narrative is seen through the consciousness of Fanny, transplanted from one home to another, so we watch her growing up, sidelined and put upon, from ten to eighteen, when the story proper starts. Equally, we observe the Bertrams as children, and see how their being accustomed to privilege in childhood shapes their actions in later life.

But the use of children in the novel's scheme of things does not stop when Fanny and her cohort of Bertram cousins reach adulthood. In Fanny's return to Portsmouth, we are plunged into the large, noisy and badly brought-up Price family, and we learn gradually to distinguish one from another. We see, with Fanny, how Sam, the eldest boy at home, is:

> the best of the three younger ones … Tom and Charles being at least as many years as they were his juniors distant from that age of feeling and reason.

This is an observation that promises improvement in each of the boys as they mature. Sam follows in the footsteps of William, Fanny's eldest brother, already manly, brave and good; Tom and Charles will follow in due course, having, as Sir Thomas later reflects, the advantage of being born 'to struggle and endure'. But it is with the daughters of the house that Fanny necessarily has most to do. Spoilt Betsey and assertive Susan at first horrify Fanny equally, until she begins to understand the family dynamics:

> In every argument with her mother, Susan had in point of reason the advantage, and never was there any maternal tenderness to buy her off…. All this became gradually evident, and gradually placed Susan before her sister as an object of mingled compassion and respect…. Susan, she found, looked up to her and wished for her good opinion; and *new as anything like an office of authority was to Fanny, new as it was to imagine herself capable of guiding or informing anyone*, did she resolve to give occasional hints to Susan…. [my italics].

Over the course of the next few weeks, Fanny pushes herself into giving far more than mere hints; she removes one longstanding source of friction between Susan and Betsey by the simple expedient of buying the latter a new knife and thus restoring the original to Susan, and more importantly she borrows books from the library to read and discuss with her fourteen-year-old sister. All this is accomplished without any encouragement from their mother. Imperfect but improvable and even lovable, Susan Price becomes a character of real interest to us (just as Margaret Dashwood, of the same age, might have been in *Sense and Sensibility*), while Fanny changes from being the youngest in a household, always under somebody's direction, to being an autonomous adult, exercising her own judgement and common sense. In this great leap forward in her personal growth, Fanny proves that she will become, in her eventual marriage to Edmund, an equal partner in raising their family.

This extended passage is exceptional in the novels, as befits Fanny's story, but in telling touches elsewhere children are often used to demonstrate the heroine's potential for motherhood. In *Pride and Prejudice*, as we have seen, it is Jane, rather than Elizabeth, who proves she will make an excellent mother – warmer, perhaps, than Elizabeth herself, though Elizabeth will bring her sharper intelligence to bear on the role. In *Persuasion* Anne Elliot is not only able to keep her nephews in better order than their own mother, but when little Charles is injured she tends to him with more care and far less selfishness than her inadequate sister.

The Musgrove boys can show as much 'tyranny' as the Middletons on occasion, and the determination of the younger to stake his claim in anything good that is going is certainly reminiscent of *Sense and Sensibility*. But the fault lies not so much in the children themselves as in their management by the adults in their lives. *Persuasion* also contains the lovely vignette of the visiting Admiral Crawford teasing the delighted little boys with offers to carry them away in his pockets.

When Emma Woodhouse has sole charge of her two eldest nephews, Henry and John, at Hartfield, she proves herself a better mother than her timid and hypochondriac sister Isabella, in so much as she refuses to give the boys what she calls 'false physick'. Just like Jane Bennet, Emma Woodhouse teaches and plays with the children in her charge – making them a set of alphabet cards and telling them the story of the gypsies, which she has to repeat word for word in every subsequent retelling. She defends her brother-in-law (usually no favourite with her) from Mr Woodhouse's charge of being too rough with them, considering it admirable that he should wish his boys to grow up active and hardy. We see Emma dancing the latest baby in her arms, and being told by Mr Knightley, with whom she has had a previous disagreement, that:

'If you were as much guided by nature in your estimate of men and women, and as little under the power of fancy and whim in your dealings with them, as you are where these children are concerned, we might always think alike.'

Another set of good parents in the making.

Throughout Austen's fiction, children not only flesh out the realities of family life and provide some delightful portraits in their own right but, in demonstrating the judicious blend of robustness and tenderness in the heroines' practice of child-rearing, suggest promise for the next generation.

# 9

# NOVEMBER IN THE NOVELS

As the nights draw in and the days get colder, what could be nicer than to curl up in a cosy room with a Jane Austen novel, or a DVD of one of the films? But Jane Austen's characters themselves, of course, have to manage without central heating, electric light and entertainment on tap. Nor are they occupied with the extensive preparations for Christmas that characterize the month for so many of us. So, how do they pass their Novembers, and does anything important happen to them during a month that has the potential of being the dreariest in the year?

Emma Woodhouse, left alone with her aged father on Mrs Weston's marriage, foresees that:

> many a long October and November evening must be struggled through at Hartfield, before Christmas brought the next visit from Isabella and her husband, and their little children, to fill the house and give her pleasant society again.

Edmund Bertram is equally pessimistic on Mary Crawford's account. He tells Fanny:

> 'This is the first October that she has passed in the country since her infancy, and November is a still more serious month, and I can see that Mrs Grant is very anxious for her not finding Mansfield dull as winter comes on.'

Fanny, who enjoys quiet, uneventful days indoors, has no sympathy with this.

As it happens, Mary's tedium is alleviated by visits to the Parsonage every few days by Fanny herself, but not because she has taken pity on Mary. Out on an errand, Fanny is obliged to take shelter from a shower of rain in the Parsonage when Dr Grant himself comes out with an umbrella. Following that first visit, she finds herself becoming, in the absence of anybody more exciting, 'a welcome, an invited guest; and in the gloom and dirt of a November day, most acceptable to Mary Crawford.' But for one character in the same novel, November brings something much worse than tedium, gloom and dirt.

That character is Maria Bertram. 'November was the black month' fixed for the return of Sir Thomas, who writes that he plans to take the September packet ship from Antigua, and to be 'with his beloved family again early in November'. His return home will herald the marriage of Maria to Mr Rushworth, which has been waiting only on her father's return.

> It was a gloomy prospect, and all that she could do was to throw a mist over it, and hope when the mist cleared away, she should see something else. It would hardly be *early* in November, there were generally delays, a bad passage or *something*; that favouring *something* which everybody who shuts their eyes while they look, or their understanding while they reason, feels the comfort of. It would probably be the middle of November at least; the middle of November was three months off.

Selfish Maria gets her just deserts for wishing peril on her father. Sir Thomas arrives early, interrupting the rehearsals for *Lovers Vows* to great dramatic effect at the end of the first volume. Mr Crawford departs, disappointing Maria's hopes. Proud, angry and impatient of the restraint of home, she pledges herself anew to Mr Rushworth. A very few weeks suffice for the wedding preparations and by the middle of November – the very period she had dreamt of having a different destiny – she is married, completely of her own volition, to a man whom she holds in contempt. His widowed mother is willing to:

> make way for the fortunate young woman whom her dear son had selected – and very early in November removed herself, her maid, her footman, and her chariot, with true dowager propriety, to Bath … and before the middle of the same month the ceremony had taken place, which gave Sotherton another mistress.

Mr and Mrs Rushworth, accompanied by her sister Julia (Maria has no wish to be alone with her bridegroom) drive directly from the church door to Sotherton, and thence to Brighton and London, and out of the novel until their actions shape its very end.

Meanwhile, the narrative remains at Mansfield in November. Before the month is out, Fanny is not only paying daytime visits to the Parsonage, but is invited there for dinner, a dinner at which Mr Crawford unexpectedly reappears, and where he first notices Fanny and resolves to make a little hole in her heart. Most of Fanny's trials in the second half of the book stem from this encounter. We know it is still November, because the day before, on meeting up with Mary and Fanny sitting in the Parsonage garden, and being challenged to scold them for imprudence, Edmund says: 'Our weather must not always be judged by the calendar. We may sometimes take greater liberties in November than in May.' The unseasonable mildness for the end of November is also mentioned by Mrs Grant in connection with losing her tender plants if a sudden frost should set in, and the turkey (which is to form their dinner the next day) not keeping until Sunday.

In *Pride and Prejudice* much happens in November. Although the month is not mentioned when Jane falls ill at Netherfield and Elizabeth hastens to see her, crossing fields and springing over puddles, arriving with her petticoat six inches deep in mud, it must be early November. We can work this out because a few days after their return it is Monday 18 November when Mr Collins arrives at Longbourn. The Netherfield ball takes place on Tuesday 26 November, and Mr Collins proposes to Elizabeth the next day. Rejected by her, he has more success with Charlotte Lucas on Friday, and departs Hertfordshire on Saturday, the last day of the month. Meanwhile, the sisters learn that Mr Bingley left Netherfield the day after the ball, having business in London, and his sisters and Darcy followed him on Thursday, returning no more that winter. 'We have not met since the 26th of November, when we were all dancing together at Netherfield,' reminisces Mr Bingley when he meets Elizabeth in Derbyshire the following summer.

Elizabeth is pleased to find his memory so exact, and Jane is even more pleased, when Mr Bingley eventually proposes the following autumn, by his confession that 'When he went to town last November he really loved me,' and only the machinations of his sisters and Darcy had kept them apart. Mr Collins, with more resentment, also remembers the month: after Lydia's downfall, he reflects:

'with augmented satisfaction on a certain event of last November, for had it been otherwise, I must have been involved in all your sorrow and disgrace.'

It is unusual for Jane Austen to give dates, but there is also one specific November date in *Emma*. 'Jane caught a bad cold, poor thing! as long ago as the 7th of November and has never been well since,' her aunt laments, reading from Jane Fairfax's letter that precedes her visit to Highbury in February, where she is to try her native air (and be near Frank Churchill, to whom she is secretly engaged). In Highbury itself, the apothecary Mr Perry says that colds have been very general, but not so heavy as he has often known them in November. By the following autumn, all Jane's and Frank's difficulties are resolved; they are only waiting for November to marry, that month marking a decent interval since Mrs Churchill's death in June. The first of the three couples to get engaged, they are the last to marry, preceded by Harriet Smith and Robert Martin at the end of September, and Emma and Mr Knightley in mid-October.

Mr and Mrs George Knightley take a fortnight's tour to the seaside as their honeymoon, but have to be back to take care of her father by the end of the first week in November, when the lawyer John Knightley, who has been standing in for his brother, must be back in London. This might seem late for a seaside holiday to us, but it echoes the Austens' own habit of late autumn holidays on the south-west coast. We know that in 1803 they were still in Lyme on 5 November, when they witnessed a great fire.

This brings us very neatly to *Persuasion,* that novel of great autumnal beauty. Although Anne is at Uppercross throughout the month of October (the Crofts having taken over Kellynch on Michaelmas Day – 29 September – one of the traditional quarter-days when property leases and employment contracts often began), it is only with the walk to Winthrop, on 'a very fine November day', that Anne waxes lyrical about the season.

> Her pleasure in the walk must arise from the exercise and the day, from the view of the last smiles of the year upon the tawny leaves, and withered hedges, and from repeating to herself some few of the thousand poetical descriptions extant of autumn, that season of peculiar and inexhaustible influence on the mind of taste and tenderness.

Jane Austen is not a writer who commonly employs metaphors, but the month of November makes one of the rare examples in her work. During the walk to Winthrop, Captain Wentworth, who appears to be in love with Louisa Musgrove, picks a glossy hazelnut, which has 'outlived all the storms of autumn', and advises her to remain as firm and strong as the nut if she 'would be beautiful and happy in her November of life.'

A few days after this walk, the young people are all wild to see the Dorset seaside resort of Lyme, seventeen miles away, where Captain Wentworth has discovered friends of his are lodging. 'The first heedless scheme had been to go in the morning and return at night'. However:

when it came to be rationally considered, a day in the middle of November would not leave much time for seeing a new place, after deducting seven hours, as the nature of the country required, for going and returning.

So they plan to stay one night at an inn. They find they have come too late in the year for any public amusements, the assembly rooms being closed and the fashionable visitors almost all gone, but the delights of nature are enough: 'they praised the morning, gloried in the sea; sympathised in the delight of the fresh-feeling breeze,' the breeze which restores Anne's bloom and beauty. When, following Louisa's dramatic accident on the Cobb, Mary Musgrove stays behind for a fortnight ostensibly to nurse her, she bathes in the sea, rather extraordinarily considering the lateness of the season and Mary's tendency to hypochondria. For Anne, however, forced to return to Uppercross, the month shows its dismal side. The cottage, denuded of most of its inhabitants, is 'black, dripping and comfortless', on 'a dark November day, a small thick rain almost blotting out' the surrounding scenery.

Throughout her work, but increasingly in the late novels, with their heightened sensitivity to the season, Jane Austen utilizes the many faces of changeable November, which may be dark, wet and gloomy as a portent of winter, or mild and smiling as the last vestiges of autumn, expertly fitting them to the moods of her characters and requirements of her plots.

# 10

# WORDS OVERHEARD

Just like a thriller writer, the novelist of domestic life must invent a series of incidents to keep her stories moving along. Everyday and unremarkable as the happenings in a Jane Austen novel might be, without a constant flow of them there would be no plot and no development of character. A device she found useful on several occasions is that of one person overhearing others talking. It is used for a variety of purposes: to begin or end a story; to give information to the heroine or to the reader, which they could not access any other way; to advance the plot or illustrate character. Sometimes the effect is comic, and sometimes deeply moving.

Because the manuscripts of the six novels are lost (except for the cancelled chapter of *Persuasion*), it is rarely that we glimpse Jane Austen in the act of thinking up incidents for her characters to enact. To us, as readers, they seem to flow so naturally that they hardly need the author to invent them – but, of course, that is not the case. One such glimpse, albeit an oblique one, comes in the letter to Cassandra in which she wonders whether Northamptonshire is a county of hedgerows. She was writing *Mansfield Park* at the time, which has Northamptonshire as its setting, so her enquiry must relate to her work in progress. But hedgerows do not feature in *Mansfield Park*. We would not know what she had intended to do with them had not she revived the idea for *Persuasion*, two years later. Now we can see that all along, she had been thinking how she might use the circumstance of one character overhearing others talking behind a hedge – something that could happen without straining credulity, yet which could be full of interest and emotion for the involuntary listener. The circumstance fits the autumn walk in *Persuasion*, and Anne's painful estrangement from Captain Wentworth, as beautifully as, for example, the garden scenes at Sotherton fit *Mansfield Park* and Fanny's place as constant bystander and silent critic.

Anne, who cannot move without giving herself away, is by this means privy to a long exchange between the man she still loves and the young woman he is now pursuing, conversation which they themselves believe private. It is not sweet nothings that reach Anne's ears, but words 'of such serious warmth' that, while marking Captain Wentworth's interest in Louisa, hint also at his continuing resentment towards herself. And while they are still within earshot, this is followed up by Louisa's revelation to Wentworth that Charles Musgrove had proposed to, and been rejected by, Anne: information that he receives with involuntary interest.

> The sounds were retreating, and Anne distinguished no more. Her own emotions kept her fixed. She had much to recover from, before she could move. The listener's proverbial fate was not absolutely hers; she had heard no evil of herself, but she had heard a great deal of very painful import. She saw how her own character was considered by Captain Wentworth, and there had been just that degree of feeling and curiosity about her in his manner which must give her extreme agitation.

By listening in to this private conversation between Wentworth and Louisa, both Anne and the reader receive impressions that the author could not convey in any other way, since the mores of the time prevent Anne and Wentworth speaking openly to one another as their counterparts would surely do today. The dramatic tension of the whole novel hinges on whether Wentworth's love for Anne will be reignited; but the problem the author has set herself is that though Anne's many virtues are evident to *us*, he must be given reasons to withstand them, otherwise there would be no story worth telling. Jane Austen maintains suspense by positioning Wentworth as (in his own mind) a wronged man and the suitor of another, yet not quite indifferent to Anne.

This wonderfully rich and meaningful scene is matched, at the end of the book, by another episode of overhearing, but on this occasion speaker and listener are reversed. Captain Wentworth overhears Anne speaking, and learns her true feelings. Again, the conventions of society prevent her telling him, or even hinting, that she still loves him, even when she has begun to suspect his heart has returned to her but that he is now held back by jealousy of another man. The author, in her revised ending to the novel, arrives at a brilliant solution whereby Anne can speak up for herself and win her lover back, yet without impropriety, without even design. Anne cannot know that she is within earshot of Captain Wentworth, writing a business letter at a distant table in the same room, when Captain Harville in the friendliest manner opens a conversation with her about his dead sister, and whether men or women forget one another first. This is a subject close to Anne's heart, and in a long exchange, generous and pleasant in tone, she argues for women's constancy. (Anne's eloquence and intelligence may be compared with Louisa's limited powers of thought and expression in the previous overhearing.)

As she speaks, Wentworth begins to write a letter of love and proposal of marriage to her:

'I can no longer listen in silence ... I am every instance hearing something which overpowers me. You sink your voice, but I can distinguish the tones of that voice when they would be lost on others....'

While it may be thought improbable that he could properly listen and write at the same time, the reader overlooks this in the deep emotion with which hero and heroine come together at last. Jane Austen's inspired second thoughts for the ending of *Persuasion* are agreed by all critics to be worthy of this novel of second chances and mature love.

If overhearing brings one pair of lovers to mutual understanding, in a different novel it starts another pair on a long career of antagonism. At the Meryton assembly, Darcy speaks dismissively of Elizabeth, who is sitting down and has been suggested to him as a partner, and is quite careless whether she can hear him.

'Which do you mean?' and turning round, he looked for a moment at Elizabeth, till catching her eye, he withdrew his own and coldly said, 'She is tolerable; but not handsome enough to tempt *me*.'

This leaves Elizabeth with no very cordial feelings towards him, but she tells the story among her friends with spirit.

The following day, when the Lucases meet the Bennets to talk over the ball, Charlotte repeats a compliment to Jane that she overheard pass between Bingley and a Mr Robinson. '*My* overhearings were more to the purpose than yours, Eliza,' she adds. 'Mr Darcy is not so well worth listening to as his friend, is he? Poor Eliza! To be only just *tolerable*.'

Since even Darcy would not insult a woman to her face, it has to be in the form of overhearing that Elizabeth is convinced not only of Darcy's arrogance, but of his personal dislike of her, without which she might earlier realize his changing feelings towards her. This overhearing, rather than just a general impression of Darcy's haughtiness, is necessary to subvert her judgement for so long.

Darcy's carelessness about whether the subject of his remarks can hear him is one kind of rudeness; another is that shown by the vulgar Isabella Thorpe, who is given to whispering to her admirers – first James Morland, then Frederick Tilney – while her friend Catherine has to sit by, forced to overhear but excluded from taking part in the conversation. Mrs Elton also stage-whispers to Jane Fairfax to shut out Emma, who is quite aware of what is being said. The highly honourable Edmund Bertram, on the other hand, makes great efforts *not* to hear what Henry Crawford is saying to Fanny, by burying himself in his newspaper and even reading the advertisements out loud to himself, much to Fanny's distress. In the same novel, there is a comic moment when Tom, watching the couples dancing and giving his opinion that Mrs Grant 'must want a lover as much as any of them. A desperate dull life hers must be with the doctor', realizes that he may have been overheard by Dr Grant himself and quickly changes the subject. Even Fanny can hardly help laughing.

For sheer dishonour, nothing matches Nancy Steele's blatant listening at the door in *Sense and Sensibility*. Edward and Lucy are meeting for the first time since the secret of their engagement came out, Edward having kept away for a few days while he works out what to do; and Nancy happening to meet Elinor in Kensington Gardens immediately afterwards, relates the conversation between the couple almost word for word. By this means, we 'hear' Edward desperately – but unsuccessfully – striving to release Lucy from the engagement by citing his new poverty. Jane Austen so arranges it that Elinor (who, of course, understands what Edward is about much better than Nancy) gets the benefit of this narration before realizing that Nancy is passing on what she never should have heard:

> 'Have you been repeating to me what you only learnt yourself by listening at the door? I am sorry I did not know it before; for I certainly would not have suffered you to give me particulars of a conversation which you ought not to have known yourself. How could you behave so unfairly by your sister?'
>
> 'Oh, la! There is nothing in that. I only stood at the door, and heard what I could. And I am sure Lucy would have done just the same by me; for a year or two back, when Martha Sharpe and I had so many secrets together, she never made any bones of hiding in a closet, or behind a chimney-board, on purpose to hear what we said.'

So much for the code of honour of the Misses Steele. Their cousin Mrs Jennings, for all her brash vulgarity, has far higher standards, as we see soon afterwards. *Sense and Sensibility* contains the most extended passage of overhearing, and the most comic one, in any of the novels. When Colonel Brandon approaches Elinor with his offer of the living at Delaford for Edward, the exchange could have been narrated very straightforwardly – but Jane Austen seizes the opportunity for humour with an audacious stroke. Whereas almost all the novel has been presented through Elinor's eyes, suddenly we are in the mind of Mrs Jennings. With her preconceived idea that it would be a good thing for both the Colonel and Elinor that they should marry, Mrs Jennings imagines, as the couple converse in her drawing room, that Brandon is actually proposing.

> Though she was too honourable to listen, and even changed her seat, on purpose that she might *not* hear, to one close by the pianoforte on which Marianne was playing, she could not keep herself from seeing that Elinor changed colour, attended with agitation, and was too intent on what he said, to pursue her employment.

Occasionally, when Marianne pauses in her playing, a few words reach Mrs Jennings' ears, which puzzle her, but not sufficiently to dent her happy fantasy. The narrator then tells us 'what really passed' and we return to Elinor's viewpoint.

As Jane Austen knew from her experience of the stage, talk at cross-purposes could be very entertaining, and this is what now ensues between Mrs Jennings and Elinor, and at some length. When the conversation arrives at a point where the deception can continue no longer, light dawns and 'both gained considerable amusement' from the mistake. So do we, the readers – amusement that agreeably varies the mood of the novel in a section that is otherwise quite sombre. (And good-natured Mrs Jennings can laugh at herself without forfeiting her original interpretation, because she still believes that the proposal from Colonel Brandon to Elinor will come.)

Mistaken overhearing is such a good device that Austen might have used it again, in a different novel. But she is not an author who repeats herself, either in character or incident. She has many resources to deploy. Amplitude of imagination and flexibility of narrative technique are both demonstrated in Jane Austen's varied episodes of overhearing.

# 11

# HOME COMFORTS

Perhaps because of the tendency to hunker down in a recession, the subject of home seems to have taken hold of our collective imaginations. In his book *At Home: a short history of private life,* popular author Bill Bryson takes us room by room through his Victorian rectory, delving into the development of domestic comforts.[6] He sees the whole of history, in fact, as little more than one long struggle to make ourselves more comfortable. The Industrial Revolution, the Agrarian Revolution, wars and uprisings, scientific progress and geographical exploration, all tend to this one end. 'We are so used to having a lot of comfort in our lives – to being clean, warm and well fed,' he writes, 'that we forget how recent most of that is. In fact, it took us for ever to achieve these things, and then they mostly came in a rush.'

The rush began in the eighteenth century, as Amanda Vickery demonstrated in her fascinating BBC TV series *At Home with the Georgians*, drawing on research among private papers at all levels of society.[7] This was the period when advances in material culture kept pace with a transformation in ideas about the home. Previous generations of the rich and powerful had seen the home as a manifestation of social status, a place to show off and exert influence over public life; while the majority of the population, of course, had no hope of making a comfortable home for themselves. But the rise of the middle class in eighteenth century Britain brought with it a more diffused desire for everything the home could provide: comfort as well as status, privacy as well as security, cosiness as well as novelty.

Jane Austen was heir to all this, and her novels are rich in reflections about the meaning and reality of home. Comfort itself is a very Austenesque concept, used both psychologically and physically. Comfort for her is belonging to a well-regulated household with the wherewithal to meet basic needs; it is also being among people with whom one is in sympathy. As Jane famously wrote to

Cassandra, after enjoying French wine during a visit to her rich brother Edward, and in anticipation of returning to the home she shared with her sister where home-made wine was all they could afford:

> Luckily the pleasures of Friendship, of unreserved Conversation, of similarity of Taste & Opinions, will make good amends for Orange Wine.

But for all the 'make-do and mend' domestic economy of Chawton Cottage, which was run on a very modest income, Jane's last beloved home was replete with the degree of comfort that a woman neat and elegant in all her ways, but moderate in her expectations, could desire. Caroline Austen, her niece, has testified to the ladylike comforts of Chawton Cottage.[8]

We often think of the home as being the woman's sphere historically, but according to Professor Vickery, the impulse to provide a good home was strong in eighteenth-century men. It was their chief means of attracting a wife, with all the advantages, sexual, social, domestic and dynastic, that the possession of a wife bestowed. In Jane Austen's fiction, no one illustrates this better than the two clergymen Mr Collins and Mr Elton. Each is proud of the home – or 'abode', as Mr Collins calls it – with which good fortune has provided him, and now all that each wants is a woman to minister to his comfort and complete his self-satisfaction. Any love involved must be purely imaginary: Mr Collins transfers his choice from Jane Bennet to her sister Elizabeth to Charlotte Collins within a matter of days, and Mr Elton from Emma Woodhouse to Augusta Hawkins in just a few weeks.

The women involved know exactly what they are doing and the marriages that result represent a trade-off; but whereas only contempt can be felt for Mrs Elton's showy style of housekeeping, the reader's respect is evoked for the way Mrs Collins quietly manages and enjoys her home. Paying the newly-weds a visit, her friend observes that:

> everything was arranged with a neatness and consistency of which Elizabeth gave Charlotte all the credit. When Mr Collins could be forgotten, there was really a great air of comfort throughout, and by Charlotte's evident enjoyment of it, Elizabeth supposed he must often be forgotten.

Clerical homes that hold out every promise of both comfort and happiness are Woodston Parsonage (the young Tilneys) and Thornton Lacey (the Bertram married cousins). Both brides are young and inexperienced in the arts of housekeeping; but, as Mrs Morland sensibly remarks in the case of her daughter Catherine, there is nothing like practice. As for Fanny Price, we have observed her recoiling from the 'mismanagement and discomfort' of her parents' Portsmouth home, and fashioning her own little 'nest of comforts' out of the meagre materials available to her in the bleak East Room she occupies at Mansfield. We can be confident that wherever she finds herself she will be able to create an environment of regularity and comfort.

The pair of young marrieds whom we glimpse embarking on homemaking *together* are Edward and Elinor Ferrars. It is a charming picture. Staying at Delaford House for the first month of their marriage while they supervise improvements to the nearby Parsonage, the way they 'choose papers, project shrubberies and invent a sweep [i.e. a carriage drive]' makes them seem like any modern couple excitedly setting up home today. As time passes, Edward, who has never had a happy home-life with his mother and has led a largely peripatetic existence since adulthood, experiences 'increasing attachment to his wife and his home'. Elinor has a good example before her, the home she has shared with her mother and sisters at Barton Cottage excelling in 'sense, elegance, mutual affection and domestic comfort', despite the limited means that support it. The small number of servants there has probably made her quite practical: 'hands-on' as we would say, though Austen shows us nothing of that, except a hint of Elinor making breakfast while the visiting Edward walks to the village. So happy are the young Ferrars in their married home that they find they have little left to wish for except rather better pasturage for their cows. Grandeur and show interest them not at all.

Anne Elliot's 'warm affections and domestic habits' will surely create a comfortable home for Captain Wentworth, who will appreciate it all the more for having never had a home of his own. It is unlikely that he will expect her to live on board ship with him, even though his sister has enjoyed doing so with her own husband, Admiral Croft.

Those heroines whose bridegrooms are already well-settled in their homes – most notably Mr Darcy – miss out on the shared pleasure and opportunity to bond of creating a home together, or of inducing admiration and gratitude in a husband. There really is very little for Elizabeth to do at Pemberley; it is already a comfortable, well-run house, but Darcy has shown his readiness to modernize, in the case of newly furnished rooms for his sister, so perhaps Elizabeth will have some scope to make alterations and improvements to suit a growing family and innovations in domestic technology in the era to come. In any case, though certainly impressed with the beauties of Pemberley, Elizabeth seems the least interested in housekeeping and homemaking of any of Jane Austen's heroines. She would have made a poor mistress of Hunsford Parsonage, even had she been able to love its master. In looking forward to 'all the comfort and elegance of their family party at Pemberley' during her engagement, she is more likely thinking of the quality of human interaction than of their physical surroundings – though the two, of course, are intermeshed.

Emma Woodhouse, a practised housekeeper, is a unique case, in that her husband moves into *her* existing home, selflessly giving up his own for the unknown number of years that Mr Woodhouse will survive. Hartfield and Donwell Abbey, though 'totally unalike', are perhaps equally spacious and comfortable in their own distinct ways. Mr Knightley is one new husband whose comforts do not increase so much as *change* on marriage. He sacrifices, as Emma is all too aware, 'a great deal of independence of hours and habits', in return for the pleasure of having her as his wife, and the hope of having his own children. Luckily, Mr Knightley does not care much about his personal comfort, but he does have one important thing to say on the subject of home:

> A man would always wish to give a woman a better home than the one he takes her from; and he who can do it, where there is no doubt of her regard, must, I think, be the happiest of mortals.

He is speaking at that moment of Frank Churchill and Jane Fairfax, and as he has yet no idea that Emma could ever love him, he admits to envying the engaged couple.

While the man's role in providing the home formed the first episode of Professor Vickery's TV series *At Home with the Georgians,* the second focused on female influence in acquiring the new material comforts that were coming onto the market in this period. General Tilney (no mean homemaker himself, boasting at Northanger Abbey every luxury and modern contraption that money can buy), in showing Catherine Morland around Woodston Parsonage, draws her attention to the fact that while the dining room and study are already fitted up for Henry's use, the drawing room is as yet unfurnished, not because means are lacking, but because 'it waits only for a lady's taste.' The General even invites her to suggest colours for the paper and hangings, and though Catherine is rather more embarrassed than flattered by his appeal, these are evidently pleasures in store for her after marriage.

Mrs Grant, a childless young wife with little to occupy her time or her heart, has filled her favourite sitting room with pretty furniture, modernized the house with fashionable new French windows, made a choice collection of plants and poultry, and created a shrubbery walk. She has little now left to occupy her, except to make sure that Dr Grant gets a good dinner every day, for which the cook is paid high wages, and which is taken off a dining table the size of which irritates Mrs Norris, who, in quitting the Parsonage, wanted the new occupants to buy her own furniture. (All that we know of the White House, into which the widowed Mrs Norris moves, is that it contains 'a bed for a [non-existent] friend'.)

In *Persuasion,* the young generation of Musgroves are much more acquisitive than the older, with Henrietta and Louisa adding 'a grand pianoforte and a harp, flower-stands and little tables placed in every direction', to the 'old-fashioned square parlour' of their parents' home, while their brother and his wife inhabit what was once an unremarkable farmhouse now transformed for their use into a *cottage ornée* with new furnishings and new-fangled 'veranda, French windows and other prettinesses'.

But it is a male character in the same novel who is perhaps the most skilled in homemaking of all the creatures of Jane Austen's imagination – a character partly based on her naval brother Frank. It is not fashion, but comfort, that impels Captain Harville to make home improvements. His 'ingenious contrivances and nice arrangements' turn the small space of his rented cottage to best account and add character to the indifferent furnishings provided by the landlord. Nor are his improvements all cosmetic: living right on the sea, he has sturdily defended the doors and windows against the winter storms to come. Altogether the Harvilles' home offers to the thoughtful mind of Anne a 'picture of repose and domestic happiness'. While the Harvilles are bewitchingly ready to invite friends of friends into their home, it is also the place of their own refuge and comfort as a little hard-up family, content with one another. This atmosphere of blended hospitality and self-sufficiency is surely what Anne will wish to replicate, though her married home will be supported by a better income.

In the novels of her later period, Jane Austen anticipates the Victorians in seeing home as a refuge – from moral contamination as well as from uncongenial people. Sir Thomas Bertram's desire to 'shut out noisy pleasures' and to confine himself to 'his own domestic circle', seated at his suggestion 'round the fire', seems to foreshadow Dickens in its retreat to the sanctuary of hearth and home. Fanny is surely the 'Angel in the House' that the Victorians came to venerate. In fear of another kind of contamination, that by social climbers and/or the middle classes, the inhospitableness of Sir Walter Elliot is based on snobbery and reflects the change in Bath fashions, from freely mixing in public places to inviting the very select few into one's home. Jane Austen seems to endorse Sir Thomas's views while deploring those of Sir Walter. But both households demonstrate a marked difference from the Bennets' habit of dining with four-and-twenty neighbouring families in the earlier *Pride and Prejudice,* or the unrelenting socializing of Sir John and Lady Middleton in *Sense and Sensibility.* Between the eighteenth and the nineteenth centuries, ideas about home were changing, and Jane Austen shows us these changes in all the variety and subtlety of which she is mistress.

# 12

# SHOELACES AND SHAWLS

Shoelaces and shawls, garters and gaiters, ribbons and reticules: a multitude of small details working on different levels makes the texture of *Emma* particularly rich and rewarding. Though minds and hearts are the novelist's chief concern, she takes care to show us that bodies in Highbury are not ethereal: they have to be fed and clothed. There is more mention of food in this novel than in any of the others,[9] and more items of apparel: not high fashion, not elaborately detailed outfits, but the necessary accessories that characters use to get by in their day-to-day lives.

For example, umbrellas. What could be more prosaic? Yet it is a couple of umbrellas that herald a marriage, a marriage that will change the lives not only of the newly-weds themselves, but of the community at large. The plot of *Emma* begins with the departure from the heroine's home of her friend and mentor, leaving her and her imagination to their own devices, with all the mischief that ensues. And the first hint that the widower Mr Weston might be becoming interested in the governess Miss Taylor as a prospective second wife is given when, meeting her and Emma out walking, and with a light rain coming on, he darts away to borrow two umbrellas for their use from a nearby farmhouse. Emma recalls this incident four years later, on Mr and Mrs Weston's wedding day. In a different sort of novel, Mr Weston's gallant speeches and Miss Taylor's modest replies might have been recorded. Jane Austen prefers to focus on the practical aspect of the encounter, perhaps to distance herself from Emma's own highly romantic flights of fancy. This is a narrator who delights in presenting the incidentals of life and leaving readers to interpret their significance.

Umbrellas in *Emma* are the mark of a man with marriage on his mind. On another rainy day, when Harriet takes refuge in Ford's shop and, to her very great embarrassment, in walks her spurned suitor Robert Martin, he does not notice her at first because he is busy with the umbrella with which he has been protecting his sister. He will make an excellent husband to Harriet. Later, 'I will see that there are umbrellas, sir,' says Frank to his father, dashing away to escort Miss Bates and Jane Fairfax the few yards from the carriage to the door of the Crown Inn. This passes for general gallantry and nobody guesses that Frank is in love with Jane, yet on a second reading it becomes apparent how attentive to her comfort he is at every opportunity.

No umbrella is associated with the selfish Mr Elton, scorner of Harriet, ingratiating admirer of Emma and eventual triumphant husband of Augusta Hawkins. His accoutrements are all for his own use, and for show. 'The very sitting of his hat' as he struts about Highbury during the period of his engagement is taken by the sighing female population as 'proof of how much he was in love'.

In a novel which keeps its feet so firmly on the ground, it is appropriate that shoes should be so often the subject of conversation. In the first chapter, Mr Woodhouse fears that Mr Knightley has had a damp and dirty walk to visit them in the evening. 'Dirty, sir! Look at my shoes. Not a speck on them,' replies Mr Knightley in his cheerful way. Miss Bates, arriving at the Crown Inn in the rain, assures the company that she has 'quite thick shoes'. Earlier, she has shown 'thanks for their visit, solicitude for their shoes' in ushering Emma and Harriet into her sitting room. As we have seen, when snow threatens to separate Isabella Knightley at Randalls from her children at Hartfield, she urges her husband to set off immediately with her, even if they have to walk half the way. 'I could change my shoes, you know, the moment I got home,' she tells him, to which he replies, 'Walk home! You are prettily shod for walking home, I dare say. It will be bad enough for the horses.'

In setting out to contrive a match between Harriet Smith and Mr Elton, Emma employs a variety of tactics – from high-flown charades to portraits until, in her final 'ingenious device', she descends to the lowliest artefact of all: shoelaces. In her scheming, Emma literally stoops. Bending down to break off one of her shoelaces and 'dexterously throwing it into a ditch' while the others are not looking is a ploy to get herself and Harriet into Mr Elton's house with the excuse of begging his housekeeper for 'a bit of riband or string, or anything', to keep her boot on. As a result, in a stroke of inadvertent cruelty, Harriet views the interior of a house that will never be hers, though Emma assures her that it will. Ashamed of what she later calls the 'vain artifice' of her deception, Emma will never stoop so low again.

But footwear still has a part to play in *Emma*. Does honest, upright Mr Knightley have something to hide when he too bends down, in his case 'hard at work upon the lower buttons of his thick leather gaiters'? The narrator tells us that 'either the exertion of getting them together, or some other cause, brought the colour into his face.' What is being hinted at here? Emma has been probing into his admiration for Jane Fairfax and how far it may lead him; Mrs Weston suspects even as far as marriage. Mr Knightley may simply be embarrassed to have his private life under discussion. Or this may be the moment when he realizes that he is, actually – and astonishingly to himself – in love with Emma. The fact that he returns more times than is necessary to the subject of Jane Fairfax's shortcomings suggests the latter cause, especially as he confides, 'She has not the open temper which a man would wish for in a wife.' Emma and Mrs Weston in their different ways fail dismally to understand him. And if we as readers choose to believe that Mr Knightley's red face has no other cause than the effort of doing up his gaiters, Jane Austen gives us leave to do so, and to remain in ignorance of his true feelings until the proposal scene in the shrubbery.

Jane Fairfax herself is subject to some public discussion of her legwear (which would probably never happen in a Victorian novel – too indelicate). The occasion is the dinner party at Hartfield, and Mr John Knightley, making an unusual attempt to be civil, is talking to Jane, whom he likes because she is, unlike the awful Mrs Elton, 'an old acquaintance and a quiet girl'. The extended conversation on the subject of letters shows the old friends in a good light, pleasant and sensible. But John reveals that he has met Jane walking to the post office in the rain, which brings down on her head not only protracted bossiness from Mrs Elton, and further suspicions about Jane's secret lover on Emma's part, but Mr Woodhouse's anxious enquiry, 'My dear, did you change your stockings?'

The secret lover is, as we eventually discover, not Mr Dixon (as Emma imagines), but Frank Churchill, who has as much delight in manipulating others as Emma herself. On his first morning in Highbury, walking about the village with Mrs Weston and Emma, the latter asks a question about Weymouth, where Frank and Jane are known to have previously met. To give himself time to decide how to answer, he hastily exclaims, 'Ha! this must be the very shop that everybody attends every day of their lives', and suggests they all go in. 'I dare say they sell gloves.' His need for gloves is evidently not very pressing, but he passes it off as 'taking out my freedom' in the place, and Emma agrees that spending half a guinea at Ford's will make him very popular. It is only 'while the sleek, well-tied parcels of "Men's Beavers" and "York Tan"' are being laid on the counter for his appraisal that, having thought out his answers, he returns to the subject of Weymouth. With a secret to conceal, and his tongue well-tied on certain subjects, Frank Churchill matches the gloves themselves for sleekness.

Frank will eventually smother Jane in jewels, delighting especially in how they will look in her dark hair. Meanwhile, if he is not protecting her with an umbrella, he is wrapping her up in a shawl or a tippet (a more elegant, narrower form of shawl for evening wear). Jane is urged by her aunt to put on her tippet to guard her from draughts as she traverses the passage between the ballroom and the supper room at the Crown Inn: 'My dear Jane, indeed you must. Mr Churchill, oh! you are too obliging. How well you put it on,' cries Miss Bates as the young man evidently steps forward to silence Jane's protests by taking the tippet and putting it round her shoulders. On another occasion, Mr Knightley, suspecting something is going on between Jane and Frank over the alphabet game at Hartfield, sees 'another collection of letters anxiously pushed towards her, and resolutely swept away by her unexamined. She was afterwards looking for her shawl – Frank Churchill was looking also: it was growing dusk, and the room was in confusion; and how they parted, Mr Knightley could not tell.'

Shawls are a regular accessory for the women of Highbury. When Emma sketches Harriet sitting out of doors, under a tree in full summer foliage, Mr Woodhouse is characteristically concerned because she has 'only a little shawl over her shoulders; and it makes one think she must catch cold.' Miss Bates makes sure her mother wears her large new shawl when visiting Mr Woodhouse on the evening of the ball:

> 'Mrs Dixon's wedding present. So kind of her to think of my mother! Bought at Weymouth, you know; Mr Dixon's choice. There were three others, Jane says, which they hesitated about some time. Colonel Campbell rather preferred an olive.'

In envisioning the domestic scene at Donwell if Mr Knightley really were to marry Jane Fairfax, Emma has some fun mocking Miss Bates' habitual gratitude:

> 'And then fly off, through half a sentence, to her mother's old petticoat. "Not that it was such a very old petticoat either – for still it would last a great while – and, indeed, she must thankfully say that their petticoats were all very strong."'

The poverty of the Bates household is apparent in the mundane nature of their clothing: from London, Jane sends her aunt the pattern of a stomacher, and knits a pair of garters for her grandmother; she arrives at Highbury with gifts of caps and workbags, useful items that she knows will be acceptable.

The better-funded Harriet, who loves to be nicely dressed and to see others nicely dressed around her, has her gowns made up by a woman in the village, and purchases muslin and ribbon – two articles that are as lightweight as her own character – from Ford's. But it is Mrs Elton who wins in the fashion stakes, being 'as elegant as lace and pearls could make her' when she goes out to dinner; playing Marie Antoinette at the strawberry-picking party wearing a large bonnet and carrying a basket trimmed with pink ribbon; and sporting a purple and gold reticule (a small fabric bag) by day. Jane Austen rarely mentions colours, so the unsuitable pomp of purple and gold in a village setting is further condemnation of the vicar's wife.

And it is Mrs Elton, of course, who on the last page scorns Emma's wedding for featuring 'very little white satin, very few lace veils'. Emma herself makes no mention of her own clothing, nor does the narrator describe any item of her apparel – except for the half-boot whose lace she so shamelessly breaks; we are given to believe that Emma is above such mundane concerns. But it is just these little matters that Jane Austen so cleverly employs to illustrate the characters around her heroine, to create a believable world, and to point the discerning reader in some very interesting directions indeed.

# 13

# THE FRESHEST GREEN

Jane Austen's use of foliage in her narratives not only marks the passing of the seasons but gives insight into the minds and hearts of her heroines.

'Verdure' is a favourite word with her. As Fanny Price says, 'to look on verdure is the most perfect refreshment', and there is no doubt that her author agreed with her. In tracking the passing of the seasons in her novels, Jane Austen is particularly alive to the joys of spring and summer foliage, and it is characteristic of many of her heroines that they look beyond their own tribulations to take pleasure in the cycle of nature. Emma Woodhouse rejoices to see the roadside elder bushes breaking into new leaf, promising a fresh start after her dire errors of the winter. In *Pride and Prejudice,* as Elizabeth nears the end of her visit to Hunsford, though her heart is full of Mr Darcy's insulting proposal of the evening before, yet as she walks 'she was tempted, by the pleasantness of the morning, to stop at the gates and look into the park. The five weeks which she had now passed in Kent had made a great difference to the country, and every day was adding to the verdure of the early trees.' The date must be the end of April, as Elizabeth stays just one week longer and, after a few days in London with the Gardiners, sets out for Hertfordshire in, as Jane Austen tells us, 'the second week of May'.

If the developing verdure of the Kent countryside is analogous to the developing relationship of Elizabeth and Darcy, albeit as yet unrecognized by her, the same natural phenomenon is present as a deep regret in the mind of Fanny Price during her three months' imprisonment in the urban squalor of Portsmouth:

It was sad to Fanny to lose all the pleasures of spring. She had not known before what pleasures she *had* to lose in passing March and April in a town. She had not known before how much the beginnings and progress of vegetation delighted her. What animation of both body and mind had she derived from watching the advance of that season which cannot, in spite of its capriciousness, be unlovely, and seeing its increasing beauties, from the earliest flowers in the warmest divisions of her aunt's garden, to the opening of leaves of her uncle's plantations, and the glory of his woods. To be losing such pleasures was no trifle; to be losing them because she was in the midst of closeness and noise, to have confinement, bad air, bad smells, substituted for liberty, freshness, fragrance and verdure, was infinitely worse.

After three months of this confinement, and under circumstances of wretchedness for the Mansfield family as a whole, Edmund arrives to escort Fanny 'home'. In the month of May, with a dejected Edmund and an apprehensive sister Susan she makes the two-day journey towards beloved Mansfield, spending much of the time looking out of the carriage windows:

Fanny had been everywhere awake to the difference of the country since February; but, when they entered the Park, her perceptions and her pleasures were of the keenest sort. It was three months, full three months, since her quitting it; and the change was from winter to summer. Her eye fell everywhere on lawns and plantations of the freshest green; and the trees, though not fully clothed, were in that delightful state when farther beauty is known to be at hand, and when, while much is given to the sight, yet more remains for the imagination.

Fanny's enjoyment of nature is not shared on this journey by Edmund, who is so wrapped up in his own gloomy introspection that 'the lovely scenes of home must be shut out'. Though she does not think of it this way, Fanny surely demonstrates some superiority even to Edmund in being able to look beyond her own concerns to the uplifting and unfailing renewal of nature. She has expressed something of the sort before, when suggesting as she star-gazes with Edmund that there would be less wickedness and sorrow in the world 'if the sublimity of Nature were more attended to, and people were more carried out of themselves by contemplating such a scene.' Edmund has been her teacher in such matters, and she his apt pupil, but their roles are reversed as the novel progresses and Fanny grows in moral stature while Edmund flails about. But after the return to Mansfield, under the quiet tutelage of Fanny, Edmund does allow the serenity of nature gradually to work its magic:

After wandering about and sitting under trees with Fanny all the summer evenings, he had so well talked his mind into submission as to be very tolerably cheerful again.

The trees here are important. Edmund evidently encounters Fanny indoors frequently as well, but it is the combination of natural beauty with Fanny's soothing presence that cures him.

Fanny has always been a keen observer of nature, noticing 'the appearance of the country, the bearings of the roads, the difference of soil, the state of the harvest' on the ten-mile journey to Sotherton; musing on the wonders of the evergreen to an uninterested Mary Crawford; and finding some relief at Portsmouth by watching the sparkling sea. This characteristic of Fanny suits her introverted nature and her limited interactions with other people, unlike Mary Crawford who sees 'nature, inanimate nature, with little observation; her attention was all for men and women.' Mary lacks Fanny's capacity to be soothed by something much greater and more awe-inspiring than herself. The greatest wonder that she can perceive in the shrubbery of evergreens is the fact that she herself should be sitting there.

Like Fanny Price, Anne Elliot of *Persuasion* is deeply observant of and in tune with nature. Her story is famously an autumnal one, and 'the tawny leaves and withered hedges' that she observes on the walk to Winthrop seem to echo her blasted hopes and declining youth; she makes the analogy herself. Yet even as Anne indulges these melancholy musings, she cannot help noticing as they strike out in another direction 'the ploughs at work' and 'the fresh-made path' that indicate the farmer 'meaning to have spring again'. Whatever the pains or follies of humanity, nature continues its self-renewal. And as it happens, Anne too is destined to have a second spring of loveliness and hope. Perhaps even of fertility, in her summertime marriage with the man she is so attracted to – Captain Wentworth.

There is relatively little of nature in *Northanger Abbey*, perhaps the most urban of Jane Austen's novels; but that word 'verdure' recurs when the Tilneys and Catherine walk to Beechen Cliff, 'that noble hill whose beautiful verdure and hanging coppice render it so striking an object from almost every opening in Bath' as they still do today, setting the city in its bowl of green. Jane Austen herself must often have lifted up her eyes to this hill when walking the pavements of Bath. When Catherine comes to leave the city, she acknowledges that the magnificent grounds of Northanger Abbey are 'beautiful even in the leafless month of March', though they delight her less than the homely apple trees – symbols of fruitfulness and plenty – at Woodston Parsonage, her future home.

Another heroine beguiled by her future home is Emma Woodhouse. One of the most memorable scenes in the novel is when Emma visits Donwell Abbey at midsummer and reflects complacently that the view from its gardens of Abbey Mill Farm, with meadows in front and a bank well-clothed in woods behind, 'was a sweet view – sweet to the eye and to the mind. English verdure, English culture, English comfort....' What Emma here seems to be appreciating is nature tamed and made useful and prosperous by the ingenuity of the English, who introduced their agrarian revolution without any sacrifice of landscape beauty; indeed, with improvements in many people's eyes. Certainly, Emma has a much warmer response to this scene than to the more dramatic, but less cultivated, views from Box Hill, which give an initial burst of admiration, but fail to sustain elevated thoughts. The union of utility with beauty is the ideal not only of Emma, but of Edward Ferrars of *Sense and Sensibility,* whose rejection of rugged wildness and blasted trees in favour of snug and thriving farms is, we cannot help believe, endorsed by the author.

One of the few slips attributed to Jane Austen occurs during the description of Donwell Abbey, when she has apple trees in blossom at the same time as strawberries ripe for picking. (Some critics have ingeniously suggested freak weather during the time Jane Austen was writing *Emma,* but that is not very convincing.) The midsummer scene at Donwell shows Emma at one with her surroundings. But this is the last moment of comfort for Emma for some while, as the unpleasantness on Box Hill the next day is swiftly succeeded by Mr Knightley's rebuke, Jane Fairfax's rejection of her overtures of friendship, the mortifying discovery of the secret engagement between Frank and Jane, and – worst of all – the simultaneous realization that she loves Mr Knightley but that she may be about to lose him to Harriet Smith. As these distresses pile one on top of another, a change in the weather not only destroys Emma's comfort, but reflects her unusually disturbed state of mind:

> A cold stormy rain set in, and nothing of July appeared but in the trees and shrubs, which the wind was despoiling, and the length of the day, which only made such cruel sights the longer visible.

Her anguish is not of long duration. The following afternoon 'the wind changed into a softer quarter; the clouds were carried off; the sun appeared; it was summer again'. Emma loses no time in being out of doors:

> Never had the exquisite sight, smell, sensation of nature, tranquil, warm and brilliant after a storm, been more attractive to her. She longed for the serenity they might gradually introduce.

She attains more than serenity: she experiences unexpected joy. Before she has returned to the house, Mr Knightley has appeared and asked her to marry him. The transformation in her emotional state is as complete as the transformation in the weather.

Mr Knightley is very wise to propose to Emma in a garden; all the successful marriage proposals that we witness in Jane Austen's novels take place out of doors. Elizabeth Bennet, Elinor Dashwood and Catherine Morland all receive welcome declarations of love on a country walk; and even Anne Elliot becomes re-engaged to Captain Wentworth outside – though, confined in a town as they are, they have to make do with Union Street for their reunion and the comparatively 'retired' Gravel Walk for their private conversation in Bath. Not only that, but all the heroines accept proposals from the men they love in the leafy months of the year. This cannot be just a coincidence; it must reflect the sense of promise that is invested in their marriages. Catherine, Elinor and Anne find happiness just as spring is arriving; Emma in July, and Elizabeth and Fanny in early autumn, at the end of a summer courtship.

As for Marianne Dashwood, we do not know at which season of the year she marries Colonel Brandon but if, among the other youthful opinions that she has learnt to revise, her 'passion for dead leaves' has been replaced by wholesome delight in the fresh green of spring and the deep verdure of summer, it augurs well for her future happiness and that of her family.

# 14

# NEIGHBOURHOOD SPIES

'Three or four families in a country village are the very thing to work on,' Jane Austen famously wrote to her niece Anna, who was attempting to write a novel. Why did the novelist find the formula so useful and how did she vary it to reflect changing times?

The neighbourhood was a very important concept in the world into which Jane Austen was born, and with good reason. At a level of society where people did not go out to work, social contact had to be made in the vicinity of the home. The unit of measurement forming a neighbourhood was determined by the distance that could be comfortably travelled 'there and back' in an evening. Whenever anyone of the right social status – that is, literate and gentrified in their manners, and probably possessing their own carriage – moved in, they would be visited by the surrounding families as a matter of course, as are the Grants in *Mansfield Park* and Mr Bingley (after some teasing of his wife by Mr Bennet) in *Pride and Prejudice*. It was not a matter of personal preference but of social convention.

Famously, Mrs Bennet boasts of dining with twenty-four families in the neighbourhood. Jane's aunt Leigh Perrot, with a country home in Berkshire, calculated that she and her husband had been used to exchanging visits with thirty families. This far exceeds Jane's famous 'three or four'. It would require a Trollope or a Tolstoy to handle such a large cast of characters and make them all intelligible to readers; Austen works to a different scale (that famous 'bit of ivory, two inches wide, on which I work with so fine a brush as to produce little effect after much labour'). Among the twenty-four families mentioned by Mrs Bennet, the only ones differentiated in *Pride and Prejudice* are the Lucases, the Longs and the tenants of Netherfield Park. In *Sense and Sensibility,* Sir John Middleton delights in gathering his neighbours together on every possible occasion 'for the sake of eating, drinking and laughing together, playing at cards, or consequences, or any other game that was sufficiently noisy;' but we get to know none of them, only the inhabitants of his own house.

In reading Jane's letters, which of course were not intended for publication, we have a much larger cast of characters to assimilate. Fortunately for us, first R.W. Chapman and then in our own times Deirdre Le Faye have annotated and indexed these families in their editions of the Letters for our better understanding.[10]

While they were living at Steventon Rectory (comprising Jane's first twenty-five years of life) the Austens were not only seeking amusement and social polish for their seven growing children, but were on the look-out for useful contacts, as well as possible marriage partners for them. (As it happens, only one of them – James – married into a local family.) With some neighbours, the Austens were on regular visiting terms: the Digweeds who rented Steventon Manor from their own kinsman and benefactor Thomas Knight; the Holders of Ashe Park and the Lefroys of Ashe Rectory; the Harwoods of Deane House and the Lloyds who rented Deane Parsonage from Mr Austen; the Bigg Withers of Manydown Park, the Portals of Freefolk, the Bramstons of Oakley Hall. With such families, they might exchange morning calls, dine or 'drink tea' and play cards at one another's houses in the evenings, and meet to dance and converse at the monthly assemblies held through the winter season in the local town, Basingstoke. Other Hampshire neighbours were in an altogether different league, and while they invited the lesser gentry, like the Austens, to the occasional grand ball, these people would never have been invited back to the Rectory: Lord Dorchester of Kempshott Park, the Earl of Portsmouth at Hurstbourne Priors and Lord Bolton at Hackwood Park. The Austens were educated and elegant enough to form part of the crowd at these private balls, but the morning after, all local families slipped easily back into their well-understood places in the social hierarchy.

Among the lesser gentry of a neighbourhood, members would expect to know everything about one another. Jane's letters to Cassandra give many snippets of news about these people. No wonder Henry Tilney, in *Northanger Abbey*, suggests that nobody can get away with anything in the English countryside 'where every man is surrounded by a neighbourhood of voluntary spies'.

There was a different little 'social commonwealth' for Jane and Cassandra to feel part of when they visited wealthy brother Edward in Kent, as his neighbours became familiar to them. Jane Austen's knowledge of human nature was honed by having all these people to study – ordinary, unremarkable people, different from those she encountered in the overblown fiction with which she grew up. Her writing, which had begun by poking fun at the sentimental creations of modern literature, began to exploit the comic potential and moral dilemmas of real-life situations and characters. Like her own Elizabeth Bennet, her lively mind found 'something new to be observed for ever' in the 'confined and unvarying society' into which she was born. Though capable of laughing at her neighbours' foibles, Jane never expressed dissatisfaction or boredom with her country neighbourhood, and it is well known that she was deeply distressed at the prospect of leaving it for Bath, where social relationships were more fleeting and superficial.

When eventually the core Austen family of widowed mother and two unmarried daughters settled at Chawton Cottage, several factors combined to make neighbourhood socializing a much less important part of their life than it had been at Steventon. Satellite households of brothers and sisters-in-law, nephews and nieces, provided almost all the company they needed and preferred. Another factor was economic: the women had lost their breadwinner, and could not afford to run a carriage or give dinners, except to similar impoverished gentlewomen like Miss Benn, who was so lucky as to be dining at Chawton Cottage on the day that the first printed copies of *Pride and Prejudice* arrived, and was privileged to hear the first chapters read aloud by Mrs Austen and Jane. Jane was busy with her novels, and the pattern of their lives had changed. A niece remembered:

> their visitings did not extend far – there were a few families living in the village – but no great intimacy was kept up with any of them – they were upon friendly but rather distant terms, with all – yet I am sure my Aunt Jane had a regard for her neighbours and felt a kindly interest in their proceedings. She liked immensely to hear all about them.[11]

This change in focus for Jane, as she directed her thoughts increasingly inward to her own extended family connections and to the creatures of her imagination, coincided with a shift in society generally. The three novels written at Steventon reflect the eighteenth-century frequency of neighbourhood socializing. In *Pride and Prejudice*, within a fortnight of meeting Mr Bingley, Jane has dined with him four times at different houses besides dancing with him at the Meryton assembly. In the same novel, during the Gardiners' week-long visit to Longbourn, they do not sit down once to a purely family dinner. In the Devon of *Sense and Sensibility*, Sir John Middleton is not the only gregarious host:

> he had been to several families that morning in the hopes of procuring some addition to their number, but it was moonlight and everybody was full of engagements.

Given the poor state of country roads and inadequate illumination of carriages, a full moon was encouragement to venture out.

In the later novels, neighbourhood gatherings do happen, of course, but they are much rarer, and therefore more significant. Sir Thomas gives a ball at Mansfield Park, to which all the neighbouring families are invited, but such a thing has never happened before. His preference is to 'shut out noisy pleasures' and he is not condemned by his author for 'wanting to be alone with his family'.

'Neighbourhood' bears quite a different concept in *Emma*. It corresponds to our own idea of the word, meaning a local community comprising all levels of society, including professional men, tradespeople and labourers, rather than a network of landed gentry across a wider area as in *Pride and Prejudice* and *Sense and Sensibility*. There are no four-and-twenty families on an equal footing with Hartfield, no dining in company four times a fortnight for Emma Woodhouse. Dinner parties are rare events and a ball still rarer. Yet in one way or another, her neighbours occupy almost all of Emma's thoughts, and she certainly likes to know and to direct much of their business – though she can be scathing about their own gossipy habits. She shrinks from being classed with the Mrs Eltons, Mrs Perrys and Miss Bates of the place; and when the secret of her engagement to Mr Knightley becomes common knowledge, the pair have great amusement in thinking of themselves as the subject of conversation in every village drawing room that evening. Before she can win her hero, however, Emma has to learn how to fulfil her allotted role in the community, not in the sense of displaying social graces (those come easily), but in behaving charitably and respectfully to everybody, acknowledging that they all have their value in a healthy thriving neighbourhood and must all care for one another. This is something wholly new in Austen's work.

And new again are the multiple examples of what the word might mean in *Persuasion*. Before the story starts, Elizabeth Elliot has for thirteen years been 'walking immediately after Lady Russell out of all the drawing rooms and dining rooms in the country' and 'opening every ball of credit which a scanty neighbourhood afforded': the traditional sense of the word, made even more socially exclusive by Sir Walter's snobbish dictates. In Bath, he regards very few of the large population as worthy of admission to his company. Back in the country, the Musgrove family are unceremonious and hospitable, much to be preferred. But better still is what Anne observes in Lyme. Here, among Captain Wentworth's fellow naval officers, she is charmed by 'a degree of hospitality so uncommon, so unlike the usual style of give-and-take invitations, and dinners of formality and display' that she has known at Kellynch.

This, then, is a different kind of 'neighbourhood' or 'social commonwealth', defined not by geography, but by professional association and congenial tastes.

English society was enlarging and fragmenting, for better or worse, and no longer would a country neighbourhood be the only social unit to which a person might owe allegiance, as Jane Austen demonstrates in both *Persuasion* and her next (sadly unfinished) novel *Sanditon*. Here she expands the scene still further into three or four families – and a clutch of visitors – coming together in a brand new, commercially active, seaside town. Characters are more rootless, more mixed, brought into relationship with one another not by accident of place, but by a restless quest for pleasure on one side and for profit on another.

As Jane Austen observed, with a growing number of middle-class people having money, mobility and aspirations to share social and material pleasures, the old elite reacted by becoming more choosy, more protective of hearth and home like Sir Thomas Bertram, more fearful of leaving his house like Mr Woodhouse, or more snobbishly exclusive like Sir Walter Elliot. All these heads of household retreat from neighbours in one way or another (though Mr Woodhouse likes to have old neighbours come to him) – very different from Sir John Middleton or Sir William Lucas, who cannot get enough of their company – even though, as John Knightley rightly says, in such gatherings there can be 'nothing to say or hear that was not said or heard yesterday, and may not be said and heard again tomorrow'. The clash of values between John Knightley, impatient of mediocrity, on the one hand, and both the sociable Mr Weston and the ingratiating Mr Elton, who while unmarried 'has more invitations than there are days in the week' according the village report, is part of the comedy of *Emma*. When Mr John Knightley and Mr Elton walk into the Westons' drawing room on Christmas Eve, the former has to smile more than comes naturally, and the latter less.

Depicted here is a society where personal preference is allowed some weight in the way people conduct their public lives. Though the Bennet and Dashwood sisters often have to socialize with people they do not much like, just because they are of the same class and happen to live nearby, in the later novels the old order is questioned, and alternatives depicted and explored.

# 15

# SHE IS PRETTY ENOUGH

In the world of *Emma*, where author and heroine alike place a high value on good manners, it is somewhat surprising to find characters prone to discussing one another's appearance behind their backs. Even in our own easy-going culture, this would seem rather a rude thing to do; in a formal society such as Jane Austen describes, one would expect it to be taboo. But in *Emma*, even the best-behaved characters indulge in personal remarks.

The most shocking instance occurs when, during a visit to Miss Bates, an ingenious suspicion enters Emma's brain that the newly married Mr Dixon is really in love not with his bride, the erstwhile Miss Campbell, but with her close friend Jane Fairfax, Miss Bates' niece. 'Mrs Dixon, I understand,' says Emma, in support of her theory, 'has no remarkable degree of personal beauty; is not, by any means, to be compared with Miss Fairfax.' To which Miss Bates replies:

> 'Oh! no. You are very obliging to say such things – but certainly not. There is no comparison between them. Miss Campbell always was absolutely plain – but extremely elegant and amiable.'

Miss Bates may be notorious for her unguarded tongue, but she is invariably kindly and polite. Emma prides herself on her gracious manners and social correctness at all times. Yet both women allow themselves to utter these personal reflections on poor Mrs Dixon. And where did Emma get her idea of Miss Campbell's being plain in the first place, if not from Miss Bates via Jane Fairfax? It seems they have all been used to discuss her unfortunate looks.

Then there is the discussion of Jane Fairfax's own appearance indulged in by Emma and Frank Churchill. On Emma's side there is a little defensiveness – she is not quite sure of her superiority over Jane, and Emma needs to feel superior to everybody. As for Frank, he has a secret to hide and a game to play; later we understand that he is, in fact, speaking the exact opposite of his real opinion. But whatever his motivation may be, whether sincere or duplicitous, he is, in fact, being unpardonably rude in discussing the looks of one female acquaintance with another. Newly arrived in Highbury, Frank has only recently been introduced to Emma and has admitted to only a slight prior acquaintance with Jane. When he has paid his first visit to the Bates household, Emma asks:

'And how did you think Miss Fairfax looking?'

'Ill, very ill – that is, if a young lady can ever be allowed to look ill.... Miss Fairfax is naturally so pale, as almost always to give the appearance of ill health. A most deplorable want of complexion.'

Emma would not agree to this, and began a warm defence of Miss Fairfax's complexion: 'It was certainly never brilliant, but she would not allow it to have a sickly hue in general; and there was a softness and a delicacy in her skin which gave peculiar elegance to the character of her face.' He listened with all due deference; acknowledged that he had heard many people say the same – but yet he must confess, that to him nothing could make amends for the want of a fine glow of health. Where features were indifferent, a fine complexion gave beauty to them all; and where they were good, the effect was – fortunately he need not attempt to describe what the effect was.

'Well,' said Emma, 'there is no disputing about taste. At least you admire her except her complexion.'

He shook his head and laughed. 'I cannot separate Miss Fairfax and her complexion.'

Frank's stated opinion that a woman can only be considered attractive if she has 'a fine glow of health' is designed to deceive Emma, Mrs Weston and even the reader, because we know that Emma herself is characterized by just such a look. Therefore, Frank must be attracted to Emma, as both Emma and Mrs Weston hope, and as the author wants us to believe. Emma's charms are known to us from a conversation between Mrs Weston herself and Mr Knightley. He has been criticizing Emma's conduct, and Mrs Weston turns the subject by remarking:

'How well she looked last night!'

'Oh! You would rather talk of her person than her mind, would you? Very well; I shall not attempt to deny Emma's being pretty.'

'Pretty! say beautiful rather. Can you imagine anything nearer perfect beauty than Emma altogether – face and figure?'

'I do not know what I could imagine, but I confess that I have seldom seen a face or figure more pleasing to me than hers. But I am a partial old friend.'

'Such an eye! – the true hazel eye – and so brilliant! regular features, open countenance, with a complexion! oh! what a bloom of full health, and such a pretty height and size; such a firm and upright figure. There is health, not merely in her bloom, but in her air, her head, her glance. One hears sometimes of a child being "the picture of health"; now Emma always gives me the idea of being the complete picture of grown-up health. She is loveliness itself. Mr Knightley, is not she?'

'I have not a fault to find with her person,' he replied. 'I think her all that you describe. I love to look at her; and I will add this praise, that I do not think her personally vain. Considering how very handsome she is, she appears to be little occupied with it; her vanity lies another way.'

This exchange is certainly useful in giving the reader a vivid impression of Emma's physical presence without her ever reflecting on it herself. More significantly, the passage offers the first hint that Mr Knightley might harbour a passion for Emma, albeit not yet recognized by himself for what it is. His disclaimer that he is just 'a partial old friend' is intended to deceive not Mrs Weston so much as himself. The fact that he loves to look at Emma is a promising first step towards admitting sexual attraction and real love, which during the course of the story, jealousy of Frank's attentions will bring to the fore. At this early stage, Austen requires her readers to think of Mr Knightley as unromantically as Emma does, for otherwise we might foresee the match too easily, spoiling the suspense; but at the same time she is planting evidence of physical admiration, so that when his proposal of marriage eventually comes, it is not seen as implausible or devoid of the motivation for married love. Given that the passage is so essential to Austen's artistic purposes, she has to rely on the reader to overlook any doubt as to whether the ladylike Mrs Weston and gentlemanly Mr Knightley would really indulge in extended personal remarks about Emma this way.

Not that this is the only occasion when Mrs Weston, kind, gentle and courteous as she is, makes personal remarks. In looking at Emma's sketch of Harriet Smith, she adds her criticism to other people's, saying that Emma has given Miss Smith the only beauty she lacks: 'Miss Smith has not those eyebrows and eyelashes. It is the fault of her face that she has them not.'

When Edmund Bertram discusses Mary Crawford's appearance with Fanny it is in a complimentary way. Pushed for her opinion, Fanny has tried to be generous by saying, 'She is so extremely pretty, that I have great pleasure in looking at her,' in response to which, Edmund enthuses, 'It is her countenance that is so attractive. She has a wonderful play of feature!' Much later in the story, Henry and Mary Crawford likewise discuss Fanny's looks. The newly smitten Henry declares:

'She is quite a different creature from what she was in the autumn. She was then merely a quiet, modest, not plain-looking girl, but she is now absolutely pretty. I used to think she had neither complexion nor countenance; but in that soft skin of hers, so frequently tinged with a blush as it was yesterday, there is decided beauty; and from what I observed of her eyes and mouth, I do not despair of their being capable of expression enough when she has anything to express. And then – her air, her manner, her *tout ensemble* is so indescribably improved! She must be grown two inches, at least, since October.'

To which his sister replies:

'I have always thought her pretty – not strikingly pretty, but "pretty enough", as people say; a sort of beauty that grows on one. Her eyes should be darker, but she has a sweet smile.'

Mary Crawford puts the other improvements in Henry's perception of Fanny down to her having a new dress, there being no tall women in the room, and Henry needing someone to flirt with.

In other novels, remarks about other people's appearance are uttered only by the vain or the vulgar. In *Pride and Prejudice*, Lydia Bennet says that it is impossible Wickham ever loved Miss King as she is 'a nasty little freckled thing', and Elizabeth is shocked to consider that while incapable of the *expression* herself, the *sentiment* is exactly what her own mind has entertained. We are thus assured that Elizabeth, with her better manners and better morality, would never allow herself to give voice to such a thought, and that even the thought itself – judging someone on appearance – troubles her conscience. The Bingley sisters talk about Elizabeth's appearance behind her back, after she has arrived hot and bedraggled from her quick walk to Netherfield; and in Derbyshire, Miss Bingley tries to make first Georgiana Darcy and then Mr Darcy himself agree that Elizabeth has grown 'brown and coarse', but they will not do so. Undeterred, Miss Bingley continues to berate Elizabeth's appearance in great detail:

'Her face is too thin; her complexion has no brilliancy; and her features are not at all handsome. Her nose wants character; there is nothing marked in its lines. Her teeth are tolerable, but not out of the common way; and as for her eyes, which have sometimes been called so fine, I never could perceive anything extraordinary in them. They have a sharp, shrewish look.'

This diatribe does nothing to ingratiate herself with Mr Darcy.

In *Persuasion*, Sir Walter Elliot is forever criticizing the looks of other people, from Admiral Baldwin's 'face the colour of mahogany' to the eighty-seven women he saw going by in Bath without a tolerable face among them. At various times he criticizes the appearance of Lady Russell, Mrs Clay, his daughter Mary and – probably, when she is out of earshot – Anne, for whose appearance we know he has no admiration, since only Elizabeth of his daughters takes after him. Anne must inherit her 'mild dark eyes' from her mother, for whom Sir Walter felt – what? No attraction? Since he cares so obsessively about looks (and rank), if he did not admire those of the Miss Elizabeth Stevenson who became his bride, he must surely have married her for her money.

When Anne tries to warn Elizabeth that Mrs Clay has designs on their father, she is met by this response:

'If Mrs Clay were a very beautiful woman, I grant you, it might be wrong to have her so much with me; not that anything in the world, I am sure, would induce my father to make a degrading match, but he might be rendered unhappy. But poor Mrs Clay, who with all her merits, can never have been reckoned tolerably pretty, I really think poor Mrs Clay may be staying here in perfect safety. One would imagine you had never heard my father speak of her personal misfortunes, though I know you must fifty times. That tooth of hers and those freckles. Freckles do not disgust me so very much as they do him. I have known a face not materially disfigured by a few, but he abominates them. You must have heard him notice Mrs Clay's freckles.'

Good manners demand that as the acknowledged – but socially inferior – friend of Elizabeth, and as the female house guest of Sir Walter, Mrs Clay should be safe from such remarks. On the contrary, father and daughter, who so pride themselves on being well bred, are condemned out of their own mouths.

But in *Emma* it is different; characters are free to make personal remarks with authorial impunity. At the end of the novel, with his engagement to Jane no longer to be concealed, Frank returns to the subject of her complexion. This time Jane herself is present, as he asks Emma:

'Did you ever see such a skin? – such smoothness! such delicacy! – and yet without being actually fair. One cannot call her fair. It is a most uncommon

102

complexion, with her dark eye-lashes and hair – a most distinguishing complexion! So peculiarly the lady in it. – Just colour enough for beauty.'

This *volte-face* attracts nothing worse from either Emma or the author than
indulgent laughter.

Uniquely among the novels, *Emma* contains no 'villain' or anti-hero to be
unmasked and banished from the heroine's life. Nobody, in fact, more unpleasant than the Eltons; and they are allowed to stay in post, as the Vicar of Highbury
and his wife, at the novel's end. It is fitting perhaps that the very last speech
within the novel is a personal remark, with Mrs Elton unimpressed by Emma's
appearance on her wedding day: 'Very little white satin, very few lace veils; a
most pitiful business!' But then, Mrs Elton *is* vulgar.

Rather than giving lengthy descriptions in the narrative, Jane Austen manages
to convey a great deal of information about people's appearances in dialogue,
thus achieving two ends: we learn more about the moral code and values of the
speakers, whilst having the pleasure of absorbing what her heroines and other
characters look like.

# 16

# SMALL WORLD

Coincidence can be an important element in the novelist's armoury, providing it is handled with discretion. 'Mrs Smith had been able to tell her what no one else could have done.' The episode towards the end of *Persuasion*, when Anne Elliot calls on an old schoolfellow with whom she had lost touch, only to find that she is the widow of Anne's cousin's intimate friend, and can give information about Mr Elliot's shady past and dubious morals that Anne could not have obtained from any other source, has been found unsatisfactory by some readers. Objections can be made on two counts. The relationship itself may seem too far-fetched a coincidence. To counter this, it could be argued that within a much smaller national population, of whom the gentry formed only a tiny part, it was inevitable that such chains of acquaintance and coincidence should emerge quite often. This is what we might call the 'small world' theory. Known even to ourselves, Jane Austen's contemporaries may not have found it at all unlikely. We will encounter it again in other novels.

The second more specific objection, the plausibility of Mrs Smith's being able to produce corroborating evidence in the form of letters, is less easy to defend. Here, surely, Jane Austen is stretching credulity, and hoping to get away with it at a point in her story where a dramatic denouement is the convention, the pace of reading quickens, and critical faculties may be laid aside in the excitement of nearing the end. Mrs Smith gives the best explanation she can, though it is a rather feeble one: the letter from Mr Elliot to Mr Smith 'happened to be saved; why, one can hardly imagine.'

We know that Jane Austen was suffering a debilitating illness as she wrote *Persuasion*, and though she completed it and moved on to begin a new novel, strangely she did not submit it to her publisher. The best explanation for this is that she was dissatisfied with her own work. If so, she is more likely to have been dissatisfied with later than earlier passages, as her weakness took hold. What is certain is that *Persuasion* begins very confidently, and very leisurely, with situations and characters promising a novel quite as long as *Emma* or *Mansfield Park*, but that it seems to come to a conclusion in a rush of quickly tied loose ends. This theory is well supported by comparing the coincidence of the Mrs Smith narrative with the way Austen handles an even greater coincidence at the beginning of the novel, without arousing the least scepticism in her readers.

Consider how we could react if we had already learnt about Anne's broken engagement to Captain Wentworth when his sister suddenly turns up as the new tenant of Anne's home. Too much of a coincidence, we would feel, spoiling the story from the start. But Austen has cleverly avoided that trap. While she gives us the outline of Elizabeth's disappointment in Mr Elliot early on, along with much other family history, she withholds the equivalent back story of Anne. We are introduced to Anne; we see through her eyes the tragicomedy of her father's retrenchments and reluctant agreement to let Kellynch. But it is only *after* the Crofts have presented themselves as likely tenants that we learn the most important thing about the heroine – the regrets and enduring love for one man, which have clouded her youth. This 'sorrowful little history' is so deeply involving that we are carried beyond the fact of the Kellynch tenancy and give it no great critical thought. It helps, too, that Anne herself does not regard the Crofts' coming as an unlikely coincidence, only as an event of painful emotion. The complex opening chapters of *Persuasion* have not always been credited with the high level of control, the fine artistic judgement, which Austen here displays. In August 1815, when she began this novel, she was surely writing at the height of her powers.

Her masterly touch is in evidence again halfway through the novel on the first appearance of Mr Elliot in person. Undeniably, it is a coincidence that he should be on the shore at Lyme at exactly the same time as Anne. But what the circumstance loses in implausibility, it gains in dramatic power. A mysterious stranger, an openly admiring glance, the rekindling of Captain Wentworth's feelings for Anne as a result of another man's admiration: all this is achieved by the clever stroke of bringing Mr Elliot to Lyme. True, Austen could have invented a passing stranger, never heard of again, if Captain Wentworth's reaction were all that mattered; but that passage has an afterlife. What Anne later thinks of as 'a cousinly little interview' – though the cousins are not yet aware of their relationship – gives them a warmer interest in one another when their real acquaintance develops in Bath. This extends to the reader: Mr Elliot interests us more, seems a more serious suitor for Anne, than if he appeared first as the protégé and intimate of Sir Walter and Elizabeth. By virtue of this prior meeting he seems to belong to Anne, and it is she who must assess his worth and withstand his pursuit. And when Captain Wentworth follows her to Bath, the jealousy he quickly conceives of Mr Elliot has its foundation in the scene on the beach. By linking Anne's Lyme experiences with those she will encounter in Bath, Austen weaves the parts of her story together. For all these reasons, this use of coincidence is artistically justified.

This passage serves to prove that without some degree of coincidence, a fictional world would not draw together so satisfyingly. A novel is art, not life, and we expect from it the unity and closure that often elude in real life, without the author seeming to manipulate the puppet strings *too* much. So we should not be surprised to find coincidence in most of Austen's novels. It is a huge coincidence that when Jane Fairfax and Frank Churchill meet and fall in love at Weymouth, they should discover that the aunt of one and the father of the other both live in the same Surrey village! As we do not see the story through their eyes, this coincidence is inclined to be overlooked; but the story of *Emma* depends upon it.

In *Pride and Prejudice,* it is a coincidence that Mr Darcy and Mr Collins, separately visiting the country neighbourhood of Meryton, should be linked through Lady Catherine de Bourgh, who is aunt to one and patron to the other, though the men are wholly unknown to one another. Darcy and Wickham know each other only too well, but the chance of them arriving independently in the same small town at the very same time is another coincidence. These are the three men who come into Elizabeth's life in the autumn of her twenty-first year and among whom – since they are all attracted to her in one way or another – she must navigate to find the most favourable future for herself. But if there were no links between these three men, while it might be a more realistic reflection of the randomness of life, the novel would surely suffer artistically. In terms of plot, too, it is essential that some means be found of bringing Elizabeth once more into Darcy's company. Would their paths have crossed again if Elizabeth had not visited Kent? It is very convenient (as well as highly comic) that the Collins' rectory is so close to Rosings, where Darcy happens to be visiting. Until his interest is reignited there, Darcy has no intention of seeking her out, and as we can be sure he would never have let Bingley get near the Bennets again, there would have been no more visiting Netherfield.

In *Northanger Abbey,* it is a coincidence that among all the visitors to Bath, the first female friend made by the heroine after her arrival in the city turns out to be the sister of her brother's university friend. That is helpful to the plot, as Isabella has already got her eye on James Morland, and her friendship with Catherine facilitates her campaign to make him fall in love with her. As a consequence, their engagement, while quick enough, is not as rushed as if they met only after Catherine arrives in Bath.

Only *Mansfield Park* seems to be without coincidences of this 'small world' kind. No one turns up already knowing someone else. (Before she comes to Mansfield, Mary Crawford has seen Tom Bertram in London, but not in any meaningful way.) No dramatic denouement depends on a revelation from the past. Present misdeeds are quite sufficient!

Coincidence of an almost melodramatic nature rules the plot of *Sense and Sensibility*. The two men who vie for Marianne's favour are linked through the offstage story of Eliza Williams, ward of Colonel Brandon, seduced and left pregnant by Willoughby. Since Eliza is kept hidden away by Brandon, and is not introduced by him into good society, there is no reason why Willoughby should ever have become acquainted with her. But somehow their paths cross in Bath. We can regard this less as a matter of probability, more as a coincidence devised by the author to give Willoughby opportunity for the heartless behaviour that Brandon can then divulge to Elinor, and thence to Marianne. It may be that, in the world Jane Austen writes about, many or most of the young gentlemen, even those who end up marrying a heroine, have at some time taken their pleasures among lower-class girls and never been found out. Willoughby picks the only girl in Bath whose protector (while signally failing to protect her) can even the score by using exposure to help win the woman he loves away from his disgraced rival. Eliza Williams' story is sad for her, but ultimately advantageous to Colonel Brandon.

To observe the unities of plot and character, Eliza is the only girl who will suffice as Willoughby's victim. As Austen writes, somewhat tongue-in-cheek, two paragraphs from the end of *Northanger Abbey*, when announcing the engagement of Eleanor Tilney to a viscount:

> I have only to add – aware that the rules of composition forbid the introduction of a character not connected with my fable – that this was the very gentleman whose negligent servant left behind him that collection of washing-bills, resulting from a long visit to Northanger, by which my heroine was involved in one of her most alarming adventures.

In a typical piece of Austen fun, these 'rules of composition' are evoked as one of the final literary jokes of that most self-consciously literary novel, *Northanger Abbey*. In subsequent fiction, she was largely to observe these rules, exploiting coincidence for her own ends, and creating the small, polished, self-contained worlds for which she is celebrated.

# 17

# DEVOTED SISTERS

The sister relationship is at the heart of *Pride and Prejudice,* giving it a solidity that transcends even the love interest. Jane and Elizabeth Bennet support and nurture each other unfailingly through the heartaches and perplexities caused by the advances and retreats of various men. We see Elizabeth at her most selfless in her feelings for Jane, and Jane would seem a blander character were it not for her genuine appreciation of Elizabeth's wit.

Jane Austen was adept at creating realistic sister pairs, reflecting the fact that birth order has considerable effect on character. So often in a pair of sisters, the elder turns out to be the sensible, reliable one and the younger gets away with being more saucy or cheeky. King George VI used to say that of his two daughters, Elizabeth was his pride and Margaret his joy. Elizabeth, now Queen for more than sixty years, has certainly shown exceptional devotion to duty and selflessness, while Margaret was more wayward and wilful (charming in youth, perhaps, but less attractive in middle age). In the present generation, the Middleton sisters suggest a similar dynamic, with Kate, the Duchess of Cambridge, showing great serenity and commitment while Pippa exercises her freedom to flirt and have fun. There is a mischievous sparkle in Pippa Middleton's eyes that would make her, in my opinion, very suitable to play the part of Elizabeth Bennet, while the beautiful Duchess of Cambridge could be Jane.

This pattern of older and younger sisters can be seen in many of Jane Austen's fictional pairs, and, indeed, in Jane and Cassandra Austen themselves. Though Cassandra remains a shadowy figure, with her side of the sisterly correspondence missing, yet everything we know about her suggests quiet good sense and composure. She was said to bear the news that her fiancé had died abroad with exemplary fortitude, which Jane admired. When they were both mature women, even while Jane's brilliance was gaining widespread recognition through her published novels, she would habitually speak of Cassandra as one wiser than herself. In one of the rare letters of Cassandra's to survive, written to a niece immediately after Jane's death and published together with Jane's letters, she says that they had no thoughts concealed from one another.

After Jane's death, young family visitors to Chawton Cottage sensed something missing, some spirit of liveliness and fun that they had grown to expect there. Aunt Cassandra, one imagines, was kind but grave. And so perhaps it is not too fanciful to imagine the Reverend George Austen, in a foreshadowing of his namesake George VI, loving both daughters but taking an especial delight in the brilliant younger one. We know that Mr Austen thought highly enough of the youthful Jane's writing style to attempt to interest a publisher on her behalf.

As for the novels, they are replete with significant sister pairs. No character is ever precisely repeated, each young woman being completely individual, yet variations on the older/younger pattern emerge. In Elinor and Marianne Dashwood, Jane Austen created contrasting but equally engaging sisters, whose story has enthralled – but not always satisfied – readers for two hundred years. It was part of Jane Austen's genius to take the commonplace novelistic concerns of her day and breathe life, wit and common sense into them. The so-called 'sentimental novel' was a genre highly popular in the 1790s, as were stories of two contrasting sisters, a prominent example being Maria Edgeworth's *Letters of Julia and Caroline* (1795). Jane Austen's first full-length fiction – first to be composed, as well as (many years later) first to be published – has as its theme the dangers of the cult of sensibility, and as its central relationship that between sisters. Cassandra Austen tells us that while *Sense and Sensibility* itself was 'begun in November 1797, I am sure that something of the same story and characters had been written earlier and called Elinor and Marianne'.[12]

Even the names of these first two heroines carry an echo of their literary inspiration. The 1790s heroines of other authors' books invariably have multi-syllable, highfalutin' Christian names, and Jane Austen spoofs these in her juvenilia with her Elfrida, Laurina and Jezalinda, among many others. After *Sense and Sensibility*, she disciplines herself to use only the names of everyday life, like Jane and Elizabeth, Catherine and Anne, for the characters of principal interest. But she gets away with Elinor and Marianne because they have a romantic mother, who may well have chosen names with a medieval flavour (Margaret, the third daughter in the family, bears the name of ancient queens and saints). The Christian names of the two eldest Dashwood sisters are so euphonious that the novel they grace was (like so much literature of the period) to have been eponymous, until the even more perfect title of *Sense and Sensibility* was hit upon.

A great title: but it has led readers to identify perhaps a little too schematically one sister with sense, and one with sensibility. To redress this, critics have pointed out that Elinor is not all sense, and Marianne is by no means without any. Indeed, the author tells us so in the very first chapter. Elinor possesses 'strength of understanding and coolness of judgement', but she also has 'an excellent heart'. In the following paragraph we read that:

> Marianne's abilities were, in many respects, quite equal to Elinor's. She was sensible and clever; but eager in everything; her sorrows, her joys, could have no moderation. She was generous, amiable, interesting; she was everything but prudent.

It is an attractive picture, all the more so when we understand that the word 'interesting' to Jane Austen meant not, as today, the opposite of boring, but something much more powerful: a quality that evokes warmth, curiosity, sympathy in the beholder. Marianne, she is telling us, is not someone whom others – if they have an ounce of feeling themselves – can regard with impartiality or neutrality. Marianne is described as 'clever and good ... with excellent abilities', but 'neither reasonable nor candid.' Candour is another word that has changed its meaning since Jane Austen's time. Now it means frank to the point of rudeness – almost exactly what Marianne is, in fact. But in the eighteenth century, it meant seeing the best in other people (like Jane Bennet in *Pride and Prejudice*), something Marianne refuses to do.

Characters and readers alike tend to *care* what happens to Marianne. Her being sometimes maddening is part of her charm. Like George VI, Mrs Dashwood seems to admire her elder daughter, but takes most delight in the younger. Marianne eventually emerges from her ordeal with her sensibility in proper subjection to her sense, but readers have been known to deplore the fate meted out to her in the form of life with worthy Colonel Brandon – all her options closed down by the age of nineteen. Leaving Marianne's destiny a little open-ended might suit our notions better. And would Colonel Brandon be better matched with *Mrs* Dashwood (another character whose Christian name is not divulged)? I have always thought so. After all, she is 'barely forty', with 'captivating manners'; Austen tells us that 'Indeed a man could not very well be in love with either of her daughters without extending the passion to her.' However, not only was Jane Austen so young herself when her first three books were composed that forty would have seemed impossibly old to her, but she was writing within a convention that demanded all loose ends be tied, all young people be married off.

Emma Woodhouse is a younger sister, much more quick-witted than Isabella, as well as more liable to be led astray by her imagination. Mr Woodhouse loves both his daughters tenderly, but it is Emma who can wrap him round her little finger. Or take the Musgrove sisters in *Persuasion,* who are very good friends with one another; they are lightly drawn in, and at first seem indistinguishable (and remain so to Admiral Croft); yet gradually we find them differentiated by the younger, Louisa, being the more lively and self-willed. Their parents indulge them both, but it is Louisa who seems slightly spoiled, and who seems as a consequence to expect to be indulged by all the world. The Bertram sisters are another variation on the theme, for while Maria is certainly not more correct or dutiful than Julia – neither sister has good morals – she is more imperious. Julia is a pale imitation. Being the younger sister can give licence to overstep the bounds of decorum – but if a younger sister does not seize this advantage, she is liable to remain in her elder's shade.

With *five* sisters in contention for their parents' approval and for success in life, the family dynamics of *Pride and Prejudice* are particularly complex. Jane and Elizabeth, the two eldest with perhaps barely a year separating them in age, are close, and share the same values. Elizabeth has 'more quickness of observation and less pliancy of temper than her sister' and is correspondingly more critical of their acquaintance. She marvels at Jane's unfeigned ability to 'take the good of everybody's character and make it still better, and say nothing of the bad.' Knowing this sister's ways so intimately, Elizabeth is sensitive to Jane's ripening love for the handsome newcomer Bingley, 'but she considered with pleasure that it was not likely to be discovered by the world in general, since Jane united with great strength of feeling, a composure of temper and a uniform cheerfulness of manner, which would guard her from the suspicions of the impertinent.' When Elizabeth discovers that Darcy has seen fit to separate Bingley and Jane, she reflects indignantly:

> To Jane herself ... there could be no possibility of objection. All loveliness and goodness as she is! Her understanding excellent, her mind improved, and her manners captivating.

Heart and mind are well balanced in Jane Bennet and she is hard to criticize – yet we cannot love her as we love Elizabeth, such is the magic of the novelist's art.

Elizabeth can be both serious and playful with Jane. She is able to rely on Jane's good sense and on her perfect probity when other people disappoint her, or when the family is thrown into disarray by a crisis. Charlotte Lucas proves herself mercenary, Mr Bingley is too easily swayed, Mrs Bennet falls apart: but Jane remains firm in her principles and consistently selfless in her conduct. Yet despite her perfect confidence in her sister's judgement, Elizabeth does not always confide her most painful feelings to Jane. This is partly to shield her from unnecessary suffering, but also because Elizabeth's thought processes range more widely than Jane's. Her mind is more interesting; this is why Elizabeth, not Jane, is the heroine of *Pride and Prejudice.* We know she is going to be the heroine even before we meet her or hear her speak, when her father says to her mother, 'I must throw in a good word for my little Lizzy', and when Mrs Bennet complains, 'Lizzy is not a bit better than the others ... but you are always giving *her* the preference', he replies, 'Lizzy has something more of quickness than her sisters.' This, of course, is a characteristic that Elizabeth has inherited from her father, and they share a sense of the absurd. Jane is not humourless – she can laugh *with* Elizabeth (sometimes despite her own better judgement), but she is never witty herself, whereas verbal wit and an irreverent outlook on life are intrinsic components of Elizabeth's charm. But Elizabeth knows, or comes to know, that there is a danger, which she must guard against, of becoming as cynical as her father.

When the newly engaged Jane, brimming with happiness, expresses the wish that 'If I could but see *you* as happy! If there *were* but such another man for you!', Elizabeth is perfectly sincere in the first part of her reply:

'If you were to give me forty such men, I never could be as happy as you. Till I have your disposition, your goodness, I never can have your happiness.'

Then Elizabeth slips into her usual dry wit, adding:

'No, no, let me shift for myself; and, perhaps, if I have very good luck, I may meet with another Mr Collins in time.'

Mr Bennet cannot maintain his front of caring little about his family and declaring them all to be silly (like their mother) in the face of the steady sense and worth of the two eldest girls. As they grow up and seek their own destinies, he starts to care about them more. On Elizabeth's return from several weeks in Kent:

More than once during dinner did Mr Bennet say voluntarily to Elizabeth, 'I am glad you are come back, Lizzy.'

When the two elder girls return from the few days' stay at Netherfield occasioned by Jane's cold, their father:

though very laconic in his expressions of pleasure, was really glad to see them;

he had felt their importance in the family circle. The evening conversation, when they were all assembled, had lost much of its animation, and almost all its sense, by the absence of Jane and Elizabeth.

And when they both leave home permanently, to become wives:

Mr Bennet missed his second daughter exceedingly; his affection for her drew him oftener from home than anything else could have done. He delighted in going to Pemberley.

There are two other pairs of sisters in *Pride and Prejudice*. The Bingley sisters are both brittle, shallow women, hardly different from one another except in that the elder has gained her husband (and is very bored by him) while the other is still on the hunt, and all the more ferocious for that. The two *youngest* Bennet girls are an unusual pairing in that it is the junior of the two who dominates and leads the way. Kitty is a feeble reflection, or follower, of Lydia, whose high animal spirits and giddy thoughtlessness are so overpowering in the family circle, and so destructive of their peace. The affection between these two is not to be compared to that between Elizabeth and Jane, being more a matter of habit and happenstance than of respect for and delight in one another's characters. Lydia likes having an unquestioning follower, and weak Kitty is easily led. Poor Mary, falling between these two pairs, has no confidante, no sympathizing friend.

One criticism that can be levelled fairly at Elizabeth is that she takes no trouble to help Mary develop into a more socially acceptable woman and a pleasanter member of the family circle, as she surely could. At such a young age, Mary cannot be past amendment, but the slightly older sister to whom she might naturally turn for friendship and advice never speaks to her unless she has to. Just as Elinor Dashwood fails Margaret, so Elizabeth Bennet fails Mary. Both heroines have the tenderest feelings for one of her sisters, but none to spare for another. Perhaps these failures of emotional connection must be laid at the door of the youthful author rather than of the heroines themselves, for otherwise in the course of their respective stories they would repent their – indifference? hostility? – and learn to help nurture a younger sister, just as Fanny Price helps Susan.

This shortcoming in the otherwise delightful Elizabeth is nothing in comparison with the multiple failures of the Bennet sisters' mother, who favours Jane and Lydia for their resemblance to her younger self: Jane in beauty, and Lydia in disposition. Elizabeth she particularly dislikes, and the feeling is mutual. As the narrator tells us in the final chapter, 'Happy for all her maternal feelings was the

116

day on which Mrs Bennet got rid of her two most deserving daughters.' Those daughters themselves retain the bonds of deep friendship even after they are married. Within a year, the Bingleys buy an estate in a neighbouring county to Derbyshire; 'Jane and Elizabeth, in addition to every other source of happiness, were within thirty miles of each other.' The conclusion of *Pride and Prejudice*, just like that of *Sense and Sensibility*, confirms the lifelong value of loving sisters.

# 18

# THEFT AND PUNISHMENT

Famously, at the beginning of the final chapter of *Mansfield Park*, Jane Austen announces, 'Let other pens dwell on guilt and misery.' With her unique lightness of touch and comic take on the world, it could be a manifesto for her work as a whole. But this novel, the first of her mature years, is, as readers have long recognized, an exception to the 'light and bright and sparkling' texture that she favours not only in her youthful compositions but right up to her last work, *Sanditon*. *Mansfield Park* certainly shares the ironic tone of voice so characteristic of this author, but it also contains a dark thread of theft, crime, imprisonment and punishment running through its pages.

Characters in this novel indulge in pilfering, purloining, scrounging and sponging. There is real crime in the form of poaching; and in the sexual crime of adultery, the only one of Austen's novels to venture into this territory. The words 'vice' and 'sin' make an appearance. There is much talk of prisons, literal and metaphorical, and even a mention of corporal punishment.

A general air of dishonesty in regard both to human dealings and material possessions pervades the novel. In one of her earliest speeches, Mary Crawford makes the cynical (or is it clear-eyed?) remark that in matrimonial transactions, 'people expect the most from others, and are least honest themselves.' Another key word is 'cheating'. When Fanny Price begins to perceive symptoms of Henry Crawford's unwelcome interest in her, she reflects that:

> he was something like what he had been to her cousins: he wanted, she supposed, to cheat her of her tranquillity as he had cheated them.

The first actual theft that occurs in the novel is by Tom Bertram, and it is not merely of some small item of passing value, but actually more than half his brother

Edmund's future income – thousands of pounds. When one considers that by the rules of primogeniture Tom will inherit almost everything and his brother very little, this theft is monstrous, and Edmund seems positively angelic not to resent it. Tom's expenditure on pleasure even before he is twenty-two years of age, when his Uncle Norris dies, has been such that the family clerical living of Mansfield, designed for Edmund's support, has had to be disposed of for a quick injection of money into the Bertram coffers. As Sir Thomas gravely tells his son, 'You have robbed Edmund for ten, twenty, thirty years, perhaps for life, of more than half the income which ought to be his.' This is a serious charge, which ought to lie heavily on Tom's conscience, but escaping from his father's presence as quickly as he can, he reflects that he was not half so much in debt as many of his friends, that his father made heavy work of it, and that the new incumbent will probably die very soon, when the benefice will revert to Edmund.

This robbery of half Edmund's livelihood is what makes all the rest of the novel possible, by introducing the alien Grants and Crawfords into the very heart of Mansfield, where the young people set hearts racing. Other thefts in *Mansfield Park* are of less monetary value, but they build to show a society where everybody – almost everybody – is out for what they can get. Mrs Norris is, of course, the chief offender here. She is forever purloining Mansfield goods, be they cut roses, or a chicken coop, or the green baize curtain from the abandoned theatricals, or the jellies left over after Maria's wedding. Nothing is too petty for her to find it worth scrounging. The scene in the coach going home from the visit to Sotherton shows her laden with ill-gotten gains: not in this case spirited away unseen like the baize and the jellies, but obtained through manipulating and flattering her social inferiors.

At the same time as indulging in this kind of behaviour herself, Mrs Norris is quick to notice and squash anything similar in others. She twice relates her 'triumph' over eleven-year-old Dick Jackson, son of the Mansfield Park carpenter, who has been sent with a plank of wood to his father at the great house just as the servants' dinner bell is sounding, but who is sharply sent on his way by Mrs Norris. She begrudges a share of food to a poor child, just as she has always begrudged anything to Fanny, despite boasting, 'Is she not a sister's child? And could I bear to see her want, while I had a bit of bread to give her?'

Mrs Norris is not the only character to take, or at least borrow, what is not strictly hers. Fanny's parents' home in Portsmouth is frequently in an uproar because five-year-old Betsey will steal her sister Susan's silver knife. The fault lies mainly with their mother for failing to teach her youngest child the rudiments of self-control and consideration for the rightful property of others. It is left to Fanny to bring peace to the household by purchasing a new knife for Betsey, leaving Susan in possession of the one which was bequeathed to her by their dead sister Mary. As well as illustrating the family dynamics and shortcomings, this episode propels timid, doubting Fanny to take an important step in her own personal growth. Without the Portsmouth scenes we would consider Fanny very much a junior partner in a future marriage with Edmund, but here we see her preparing herself to bring up the next generation and to do it well.

In *Mansfield Park*, as in all Austen's novels, the few objects mentioned have a significance beyond adding realistic detail to the scene. The silver knife and the gold necklace play their part in the moral drama. When Mary Crawford kindly urges Fanny to select a necklace from her trinket box she has to say everything she can think of 'to obviate the scruples which were making Fanny start back at first with a look of horror.' Fanny longs to know which might be the least valuable. How unlike Mrs Norris! Having accepted the one Mary seems most inclined to give away, only to find it was once the gift of her brother, Fanny's horror and scruples are renewed, to the amusement of Mary, who asks her, 'Do you think Henry will claim the necklace as mine, and fancy you did not come honestly by it?' Fanny's honesty is, in fact, unimpeachable. When at Portsmouth Henry tells her she has been there a month and she counters this with 'No, not quite a month. It is only four weeks tomorrow since I left Mansfield.' He replies, 'You are a most accurate and honest reckoner. I should call that a month.'

Mary Crawford cannot be accused of trying to steal Edmund away from Fanny because she is wholly unaware of Fanny's attachment; but Mary does purloin something that is considered to be Fanny's, if only temporarily. This is Edmund's mare, which is regarded as being for Fanny's use whenever she wants to ride. Though she knows this, Mary engrosses the animal for four successive days, depriving Fanny of the exercise on which her health depends. On balance, however, Mary's actions, and indeed her nature, are more generous than acquisitive, notwithstanding her sense of entitlement to a large income. Any hurt she does to Fanny is inadvertent and she often goes out of her way to be kind to her.

Inadvertence is not a characteristic of her brother who, before he sets out to make 'a little hole in Fanny Price's heart' – and what a violent metaphor that is – quite deliberately and carelessly wounds the peace of mind of Mr Rushworth, Julia and ultimately Maria. And if Mr Crawford steals Maria from Mr Rushworth – during her engagement her love, and after her marriage her body – Maria in a sense steals Mr Crawford from Julia. For, as the narrator tells us in Chapter 5, 'Miss Bertram's engagement made him in equity the property of Julia, of which Julia was fully aware.' But it is the adultery – an act then known in legal parlance as 'criminal conversation' – of Mr Crawford and Mrs Rushworth, that constitutes the most reprehensible crime in this or any other published novel by Jane Austen.

The authorial voice terms it 'this sin of the first magnitude'.

When the news bursts on Fanny, it is by means of a report in her father's newspaper – and his reaction is to say:

> 'I don't know what Sir Thomas may think of such matters; he may be too much of the courtier and fine gentleman to like his daughter the less. But by God, if she belonged to me, I'd give her the rope's end as long as I could stand over her. A little flogging for man and woman too would be the best way of preventing such things.'

Elsewhere only in *Pride and Prejudice*, with the casual report of the flogging of a soldier, is corporal punishment mentioned by Austen. Mr Price is a coarse man, used to naval ways (and Jane's sailor brother Frank frequently had his men flogged), but Mr Price's solution to immorality in civilian life, and especially in women, does seem extraordinarily violent.

Fathers still feel responsible even for married daughters. Sir Thomas's first response is to rush to London in the hope of discovering Maria and 'snatching her from further vice, though all was lost on the side of character'. The word 'vice' seems strong to us, but Admiral Crawford has been described as 'a man of vicious conduct' because he keeps a mistress.

The word 'punishment' beats like a drum through the final chapter. Maria's disappointment in her hope of marriage with Henry renders:

> her temper so bad, and her feelings for him so like hatred, as to make them for a while each other's punishment, and then induce a voluntary separation.

Mr Rushworth's punishment – for being stupid – 'followed his conduct, as did a deeper punishment, the deeper guilt of his wife'. Poor Mr Rushworth is the unlucky victim of two kinds of theft. His game birds are stolen by poachers, and his wife by Mr Crawford.

The wronged husband is released to take his chances with a second marriage, but there is no second chance for the wife. At the age of barely twenty-two, 'she must withdraw ... to a retirement and reproach which could allow no second spring of hope or character.' Sir Thomas forbids her his home and she is forced to live far away from Mansfield and from society with only her Aunt Norris for companionship where, the narrator tells us, 'it may reasonably be supposed that their tempers became their mutual punishment'.

It is interesting that in *Pride and Prejudice* Mr Bennet has the same first reaction to Lydia's sexual transgression, but he is persuaded to receive her by his elder daughters. Not that they take Lydia's offence lightly, but they think she should be given every chance to become a respectable married woman. We can appreciate that pre-marital sex, especially when corrected by marriage, is a lesser offence than adultery, which is breaking vows, but the difference in the respective fathers' actions may also be explained by the later composition of *Mansfield Park* and the increasing religiosity of the times. Whereas Mr Collins' advice to Mr Bennet to cast off his unworthy daughter is deemed by the narrator and the heroine as unchristian, the rise of the Evangelicals by 1814 seems to make a more severe approach the norm.

Austen the narrator fearlessly laments that it is only women who pay the price for sexual transgression in terms of social ostracism. 'That punishment, the public punishment of disgrace, should in just measure attend [Mr Crawford's] share of the offence is, we know, not one of the barriers which society gives to virtue,' she tells us in a rare protest about the double standard. 'In this world, the penalty is less equal than can be wished; but without presuming to look forward to a juster appointment hereafter,' – she means in Heaven, not, as some readers have assumed, in more enlightened times – 'we may fairly consider a man of sense like Henry Crawford to be providing for himself no small portion of vexation and regret.'

Edmund is shocked that what he regards as 'vice' is termed by Mary Crawford mere 'folly': the folly of allowing themselves to be found out. For their moral flaws, both Henry and Mary – characters as clever and charming as any in Jane Austen – find themselves cast out of the paradise that is the cleansed and purified Mansfield Park, and readers will discuss for ever whether they deserve the punishment meted out to them.

# 19

## HEROES AND HUSBANDS

In romantic novels, men are heroes before they are husbands. In most of Jane Austen's novels, we can see why the heroines fall in love with the men whom they will marry. It is more problematic in *Sense and Sensibility* because the two men who fill those roles are less immediately attractive.

It is Willoughby who turns out to be the villain of the story, abandoning not only Marianne who loves him, but Eliza Williams whom he has made pregnant; yet it is Willoughby who *appears* to have all the credentials of a hero. Marianne certainly thinks so. 'His person and air were equal to what her fancy had ever drawn for the hero of a favourite story.' She is in love with him almost before he has deposited her, rain-soaked, crimson-faced and unable to stand, in a chair in the cottage parlour. 'Her imagination was busy, her reflections were pleasant, and the pain of a sprained ankle was disregarded.' As readers, however, we join with the prudent Elinor in reserving judgement: we have met too many charming scoundrels in novels to trust as readily as Marianne.

Yet I wonder how many pick up that he is playing a part right from the beginning, when all seems to be going so well for Marianne:

She proceeded to question him on the subject of books; her favourite authors were brought forward and dwelt on with so rapturous a delight that any young man of five and twenty must have been insensible indeed, not to become an immediate convert to the excellence of such works, *however disregarded before*. Their taste was strikingly alike. The same books, the same passages were idolised by each; or, if any difference appeared, any objection arose, it lasted no longer than till the force of her arguments and the brightness of her eyes could be displayed. *He acquiesced in all her decisions, caught all her enthusiasm.* [My italics.]

But the most important male characters in the long run must be those who take into their keeping the happiness of young women we have come to care for. As husbands for the heroines, Edward Ferrars and Colonel Brandon have both been found disappointing by many readers. One thing they have in common is that, unlike most of Austen's heroes, they have both been in love before. Also unusual among Austen heroes is that Edward is known to us by his Christian name. With the exception of Edmund Bertram, who is, of course, Fanny's cousin, all the heroes are known by their surnames – sometimes, but not always, with their rank or 'Mr' attached. Edward Ferrars has only a loose family link to Elinor – slightly looser, in fact, than Mr Knightley has to Emma – yet he takes his place in the thoughts and speech of the heroine, and the minds of readers, as 'Edward' from the very first. This gives him a homely, almost a brotherly, but certainly an anti-heroic cast compared with, say, Willoughby, Wickham, Bingley or Darcy, all of whom are exciting strangers, men whose first names we know, but rarely hear.

Then again, Edward is not strikingly or immediately attractive. He has no special 'graces of person or address. He was not handsome and his manners required intimacy to make them pleasing'. The Dashwood women, indeed, taking trouble to get to know him, do soon find him pleasing in his quiet, unobtrusive way. 'Of his sense and goodness,' Elinor says, 'no one can, I think, be in doubt.' Yet the very calmness of her praise, the lukewarm terms she sometimes uses in describing him, though they have their foundation in her doubt of his intentions and her own cautious character, may influence readers against him.

Such readers have their mouthpiece in Marianne, who has not yet met her own hero but has preconceived ideas of what a young man should be. 'Edward is very amiable, and I love him tenderly,' she allows before adding:

> 'But yet – he is not the kind of young man; there is something wanting – his figure is not striking; it has none of that grace which I should expect in the man who could seriously attach my sister.'

In the 1995 film the role is taken by the very handsome Hugh Grant. No problem in seeing why Elinor falls in love with *him*! The other change made by the film is in developing the character of Margaret, and part of Edward's appeal is his treatment of the child. His behaviour towards her is playful and natural. He has a sense of fun, and he is kind. As Elinor observes him with her sister, she falls in love. He will make an excellent father. The film is an advance on the novel in this respect.

But in the novel, what constitutes Edward's real worth includes his strict moral code, which prevents his breaking his engagement to a woman whom he no longer loves, and cannot even respect. Such a marriage, if carried through, would be as bad as or even worse than Mr Bennet's in *Pride and Prejudice*. To marry with feelings almost of contempt seems to us deeply wrong, but in Austen's society, abandoning a woman to whom one has made promises is unthinkable to a man of honour. Edward, therefore, is even more flawed as a hero, having been silly enough to fall for a nasty, scheming woman; but in sticking to her against the interests of his own happiness, he is all the more valuable as a human being.

Indeed, we can sum up Edward by saying that though he is not dashing or sexy, like a Willoughby or a Darcy or even a Captain Wentworth, he is trustworthy, modest and honourable. His partnership with Elinor will be one of mutual confidence and respect. Nor must it be forgotten that Edward, who often has good reason to be glum, is, in fact, possessed of a dry, self-deprecating sense of humour, demonstrated in some of his conversations with Marianne, with whom he develops a delightful, teasing, brotherly relationship.

Elinor has had the perception to detect Edward's real worth beneath his plainness and diffidence, and she has stood by him when another woman might have been affronted by the revelation of a pre-engagement. She cannot *un*-love him just because he made a youthful mistake; his plight even brings forth more tenderness and understanding on her part. Elinor deserves a good husband, and that is what she gets. The picture of the newly married pair creating their home together, even so far as choosing wallpaper and lamenting the delays of workmen, is a very attractive one. Edward's gloom dissipates with marriage. He experiences 'an increasing attachment to his wife and home', which shows itself in 'the regular cheerfulness of his spirits'. We are at liberty to imagine Mr and Mrs Ferrars as being rather like Jane Austen's own parents, busy with their family, farm and parish, equal partners in every enterprise and mutually devoted.

But if readers can accept Edward for Elinor, and believe in the contentment of their marriage, they have more difficulty in accepting Colonel Brandon for Marianne. Partly this is due to the author's phrasing. She tells us that Mrs Dashwood, Elinor and Edward each feel a sense of obligation towards Colonel Brandon, who has done them all favours, as well as sympathy for his past sorrows, 'and Marianne, by general consent, was to be the reward of all'. This is not how we, today, like to view marriage; Marianne is a person, not a reward. 'In Marianne he was consoled for every past affliction.' Again, this is putting Marianne's own feelings at naught. It is all very well for the author to go on to tell us that Marianne could never love by halves and that her whole heart, in time, became as much devoted to her husband as it had once been to Willoughby. This may be psychologically true enough of an ardent but now more thoughtful woman like Marianne. Nevertheless, we cannot help feeling that she has had no choice in the matter, and that her options have been closed down at nineteen.

Colonel Brandon certainly does not appear in the role of hero when we first meet him. He has many of the same low-key defects as Edward: 'He was silent and grave' and 'his face was not handsome'. Less promising still, in the eyes of Marianne and Margaret he is 'an absolute old bachelor, for he was on the wrong side of five and thirty', and Marianne further mocks him for admitting to wearing a flannel waistcoat to keep out the damp. Nothing could be less pre-possessing than Colonel Brandon's flannel waistcoat. Is there any other hero in literature who wears such an unromantic garment? It certainly does not compare with Willoughby's shooting-jacket, 'of all manly dresses … the most becoming'.

Colonel Brandon is given no Christian name, and even worse, he is given no conversation with Marianne at any point in the story. How can we tell how they will get on together, when we have not even heard them converse? There has been no exchange of opinions between them, no banter, no confidences. Compare this with the number of conversations between, for example, Elizabeth and Darcy, Catherine and Henry Tilney, Emma and Mr Knightley. We are shown how these couples learn, through talking, to understand one another. Colonel Brandon speaks a lot with Elinor – and speaks very feelingly – but as far as Marianne is concerned, he just seems to follow her with his eyes. Given the difference in age, this can induce a slight feeling of queasiness in the reader. And the fact that he is constantly reminded by her of a former love, calls into question his sense of Marianne's individuality.

On the other hand – and now let us put the case *for* him – what a brave and selfless hero Colonel Brandon fundamentally is! He has done things that no other Austen male character comes anywhere near. Duelling, for a start – all the more romantic for being then illegal. He has seen active service abroad. He has been within a few hours of eloping to Scotland with his father's ward; and has sought out and rescued a fallen woman – the same unhappy woman whom he has loved all his life. This back story is worthy of a Heathcliff or a Rochester, and if Marianne had known it when she was introduced to Brandon, she might have found his gloomy looks and grave silences fascinating rather than dull. Certainly, in the film, Alan Rickman plays the part as the strong silent type with a powerful attraction for a female audience.

So when considered by the light of literary convention, Colonel Brandon hardly short-changes as a hero; and as a husband we cannot doubt that he will be all tenderness and fidelity to Marianne. He has shown, in the case of his cousin, that his heart once given is given for life – just what Marianne approves. And Jane Austen takes care to assure us that Marianne's regard (not yet *love*, note) and society 'restored his mind to animation and his spirits to cheerfulness'. As happily married men, both Edward and Brandon lose the moroseness that earlier circumstances induced in them, and which made them appear so deficient as heroes.

Among Colonel Brandon's real virtues is his consistent concern for, and unselfish service to, vulnerable women. However, this might result in one slight problem in Marianne's marriage that the author does not address. Colonel Brandon has taken upon himself the financial upkeep and moral care of the second Eliza Williams (illegitimate daughter of his old love) and her own illegitimate child. This child is Willoughby's. Its presence – even in the background – in the lives of the Brandons will be a constant reminder of the past to Marianne.

As for Willoughby, he makes not a bad husband after all. While never ceasing to regret the loss of Marianne, and to envy Colonel Brandon, he is not inconsolable, and manages to rub along with the woman he has married for her wealth.

> His wife was not always out of humour, nor his home always uncomfortable;
> and in his breed of horses and dogs, and in sporting of every kind, he found
> no inconsiderable degree of domestic felicity.

The books and music he had shared with Marianne seem to play no part in this marriage. With her he would have been happy *and* rich, as he is aware himself. But as we know from another novel, Austen does not care to dwell on guilt and misery, and she lets him find what comfort he can. Whether this includes further sexual adventuring, or whether he is a reformed character in that respect, she does not choose to make explicit.

# 20

# ONLY A GRANDMOTHER

When the shallow and worthless Honourable John Yates introduces the acting bug to Mansfield Park, he comes directly from an aborted performance at the home of another friend, Lord Ravenshaw. The play, *Lovers Vows,* was within two days of representation when the sudden death of one of the nearest connections of the family destroyed the scheme and dispersed the performers. 'To be sure, the poor old dowager could not have died at a worse time,' laments Mr Yates, wishing the news could have been suppressed for three days. 'And being only a grandmother, and all happening two hundred miles off, I think there would have been no great harm.'

Listening to this sad tale, Tom Bertram sympathizes, makes a pun on the title of another play of the period, *My Grandmother,*[13] and hopes Lord Ravenshaw may find some comfort in being able to re-absorb the jointure paid to the old lady back into his own estate.

'Only a grandmother.' How important was this relation, and that of grandfather, in Jane Austen's imaginative world? She herself did not know any of her grandparents. Her father, George Austen, was orphaned at an early age. Her mother, Cassandra Leigh, lost her own father shortly before she married, and her mother a few years afterwards, seven years before Jane (who was given her name) was born.

Perhaps for this reason, there are very few three-generational families in Jane Austen's fiction. None of the heroes or heroines has a living grandparent, though it would be entirely feasible, from the point of view of age, for them to do so. A person in their twenties, whose parents are in their forties or fifties, could very well – even in the eighteenth century – have a grandparent alive in their seventies or eighties. One such family grouping, briefly glimpsed on the streets of Bath, is that of old Sir Archibald Drew and his grown-up grandson, naval acquaintance of Admiral Croft. But Jane Fairfax, in *Emma*, is the only major character to possess a living grandparent, though the middle generation, her own parents, are both dead.

Although life *expectancy*, at birth, was so much lower at that period than now, once the perils of infancy and childhood – and, in the case of women, child-bearing – had been survived, life *span* was not so very different. As we know, most of Jane's own siblings lived into their eighties, one until ninety. Her own parents became grandparents many times over during their lifetimes. Mrs Austen, who reached the age of eighty-seven, had thirty-one grandchildren living at the time of her death (two others had died in infancy) and a remarkable nine-teen great-grandchildren. There were to be no fewer than one hundred and one great-grandchildren descended from George and Cassandra, but, of course, the majority were born after their deaths. Jane Austen lived to see her mother become a great-grandmother to Anna Lefroy's first two little girls. But she certainly has no *four*-generational families in her fiction.

In her *three*-generational families, with the exception of Jane Fairfax, the third generation consists of young children. A good example is the Musgrove family. Mr and Mrs Musgrove are parents of an unspecified number of children, of whom Charles, in his mid-twenties, is the eldest, and 'the much-petted Master Harry' is the youngest, still at school. Charles has been married five years, and has two boys of four and two. So there is very little gap between the last of their own brood of children and the first of their grandchildren. They pass seamlessly from parenting young children to being grandparents.

With so much experience, no wonder Mrs Musgrove feels that she knows better than her daughter-in-law how to bring up children. The criticisms and counter-criticisms of the two Musgrove mothers, young and old, funnelled through the reluctant, peace-making Anne, are among the comic passages of the novel. Even more memorable, the jolly, noisy Christmas scene in which an unspecified number of children from both generations, augmented by small Harvilles, cluster round laden tables and a roaring fire under the indulgent gaze of the elder Musgroves, anticipates the Dickensian cult of Christmas. Jane Austen herself, while terming it 'a fine family piece' seems ambivalent about such pleas-ures, and they are certainly not to the taste of the more intellectual Lady Russell. But Lady Russell is not related to the Musgroves, and cannot be expected to share their fondness. Little Charles' and Walter's other grandparent – Sir Walter Elliot – takes no interest in his grandchildren during the whole course of the novel, not even including them in his enquiries when he asks after their mother, Mary. Besides his habitual self-centredness, perhaps he would rather forget that he is old enough to be a grandparent by ignoring their existence.

The different generations of Musgroves live within half a mile of each other, and are as often to be found in each other's houses as their own. (Sensible Anne thinks this is not very conducive to family harmony.) A three-generational family with a greater physical distance (16 miles, in fact) between them consists of Mr Woodhouse at his home of Hartfield in Surrey and Mr and Mrs John Knightley, their five children Henry, John, Isabella, George and baby Emma, in London. The family have been in the habit of spending all their summer and Christmas holidays with their relations in Surrey, until the habit is broken just before the story starts by the need to take their children to the seaside, principally for the effect of sea-bathing on little Bella's health. But they pay their usual Christmas visit – not long enough to suit Mr Woodhouse – and in the spring, John Knightley brings his two oldest boys and leaves them with their aunt and grandfather for an extended visit.

Unlike Sir Walter Elliot, Mr Woodhouse is a fond grandfather of his small grandsons. He is so pleased and flattered that the eldest was named after himself that he continues to talk about it six years on. In a charming illustration of the pleasure grandparents can derive from their grandchildren, and of grandparents' tendency to think no grandchildren were ever so clever as their own, he tells Harriet Smith:

'Henry is a fine boy, but John is very like his mamma. Henry is the eldest; he was named after me, not after his father. John, the second, is named after his father. Some people are surprised, I believe, that the eldest was not, but Isabella would have him called Henry, which I thought very pretty of her. And he is a very clever boy indeed. They are all remarkably clever; and they have so many pretty ways. They will come and stand by my chair and say, "Grandpapa, can you give me a bit of string?" and once Henry asked me for a knife, but I told him knives were only made for grandpapas.'

*Emma* is the only Jane Austen novel in which the affectionate names *grandpapa* and *grandmamma* appear. *Grandpapa* occurs four times, with the more formal *grandfather* not at all. The word *grandmother* occurs nine times, always in relation to Mrs Bates, but this is exceeded by the occurrence of *grandmamma* thirteen times. Only two of these are actually spoken by Jane Fairfax. She uses the term once when she insists to the interfering Mrs Elton that her grandmamma's servant can fetch their letters (and she is quite correct in assigning the servant to *Mrs* Bates, even though it seems to be *Miss* Bates who runs the household); and once in a snatch of reported speech, relayed by Miss Bates, in which Jane marvels at her grandmamma's eyesight. But the vast majority of the instances of *grandmamma* are heard from Miss Bates' mouth, in speaking of her mother to Jane: 'I ran home, as I said I should, to help grandmamma to bed,' for example, or 'the evening is closing in, and grandmamma will be looking for us.' Miss Bates' affection for both her mother and her niece are reflected in this terminology: affection which Jane might experience sometimes as a bath of warm security, and at other times as infantilization and stultification. As for Mrs Bates in the role of grandmother, being past almost everything except tea and quadrille, and half the time unaware of what is going on, she is by the time the novel starts the gentlest of presences in Jane Fairfax's life. Dozing in the corner without the use of her broken spectacles, she is no hindrance at all to Frank's courtship of Jane.

In *Sense and Sensibility* there are two grandmothers, who in one scene get into competition with each other. The occasion is a dinner party given by Mr and Mrs John Dashwood in their Harley Street home. When the females of the party retire to the drawing room after dinner, only one subject of conversation engages them until coffee comes in: the comparative heights of Harry Dashwood and Lady Middleton's second son William, who are nearly of the same age. As only Harry is present, it has to be conjecture.

> The two mothers, though each really convinced that her own son was the tallest, politely decided in favour of the other. The two grandmothers, with not less partiality, but more sincerity, were equally earnest in support of their own descendant.

It is amusing that the rules of politeness allow grandmothers (at one remove) but not mothers to speak in praise of their offspring – which is probably still true today, showing how acute was Jane Austen's appreciation of social niceties.

One of these grandmothers is Mrs Ferrars, whose observed interaction with her only grandchild, Harry Dashwood, is limited to this boast. The other is the much more warm-hearted Mrs Jennings. Though she makes a lengthy visit to Barton Park, presumably to enjoy the company of her elder daughter and her three Middleton grandchildren, John, William and the atrociously spoilt Anna Maria, we see Mrs Jennings in action as a grandmother chiefly when her second daughter, Charlotte Palmer, gives birth during the course of the novel. This event is 'highly important to Mrs Jennings's happiness' and, spending the next two weeks largely at her daughter's bedside, she is 'full of delight and importance, attributing Charlotte's well doing to her own care.' As for her new grandson, Mrs Jennings can 'plainly perceive, at different times, the most striking resemblance between this baby and every one of his relations on both sides.' The only thing to ruffle her satisfaction is that the baby's father, the teasing Mr Palmer, not only claims to find his son and heir 'like every other baby of the same age', but cannot even be brought to acknowledge 'the simple proposition of its being the finest child in the world', a proposition that Charlotte and her mother plainly feel is self-evident.

Mrs Jennings is a besotted grandmother, but also a practical and experienced one, not easily panicked. About two and a half weeks after the birth, she has this to narrate to the Dashwood sisters (strangely using the impersonal pronoun for her grandson):

> 'When I got to Mr Palmer's, I found Charlotte quite in a fuss about the child. She was sure it was very ill – it cried, and fretted, and was all over pimples. So I looked at it directly, and "Lord! My dear," says I, "it is nothing in the world but the red-gum," and nurse said just the same. But Charlotte, she would not be satisfied, so Mr Donovan was sent for; and luckily he happened to be just come in from Harley Street, so he stepped over directly, and as soon as ever he saw the child, he said just as we did, that it was nothing in the world but the red-gum, and then Charlotte was easy.'

Jane Austen gives us a small number of grandparents, but whether loving or indifferent, they are all convincing in their individual ways. They add depth and texture to her portrayals of family life; and if her heroes and heroines are without this supportive relationship, it may be because their *parents* (where they have any) often themselves have lessons to learn, character errors to correct. Mothers in Austen tend to be dead, distant or dysfunctional; fathers are equally and variously flawed. An even older, wiser generation would dilute the difficulties that the heroes and heroines have to overcome on their own merits without much guidance from those whose experience of life is so much greater.

# 21

# DEAR MARY

Dear Mary Crawford,
As one of your warmest admirers, I am always so sorry when you find yourself shut out from Mansfield at the end of the novel. Every time I re-read I hope it might just turn out differently, but it never does. Two hundred years have now passed and you are still denied a happy ending. I wonder why you should be punished, not rewarded, for your delightful personality?

Elizabeth Bennet, who is so very like you, gets her man, so why can't you? You two share many traits. You both have sparkling dark eyes, a light tripping figure, a witty tongue and an irreverent attitude. But she is regarded by her author 'as delightful a creature as ever appeared in print' while your very similar charms are always slightly suspect. Your author seems to hold you at arm's length for fear of your subverting her design for her novel.

Of course, some of it is your own fault, for falling in love with a ditherer. If Edmund had proposed to you when he came back from ordination and found you still in the village, ready to speak to him very pleasantly despite his errand, all would have been settled very satisfactorily. Despite his slightly stodgy personality, I think he would have made you a good husband. You two would have settled down together and, as even your author has to admit, you would have grown more like one another as the years went on. You would have adopted some of his opinions, and when he got too serious, he would have benefited from being gently teased by his charming wife, especially as there was never anything coarse or sharp in your verbal repartee. As a couple, you would have been very much like Elizabeth and Darcy, in fact.

It must be galling for you to see little Fanny Price succeed where you failed. You never thought of her as a love rival, and to be quite honest, whatever her own secret desires may have been, I don't think Edmund ever *could* love her the way he loved you. It's not that easy to change cousinly love into conjugal love, despite any amount of sitting under trees and telling yourself that you now prefer light eyes. The physical attraction Edmund felt for you was palpable to all who read your story. He loved to observe the play of your features, and he was thrilled when you took his arm and he felt physical contact with you for the first time. Of course, men are often misled by their eyes into marrying very silly wives, but that would not have been the case with you two. Edmund also appreciated your cleverness, obligingness, quick wits and alluring conversation. He would never have found you boring as a wife. And think how he would have enjoyed listening to you play the harp when he relaxed in the evening after a hard day's sermonising or sick-visiting his parishioners.

All that held him back from following his heart were some rather ridiculous scruples. You spoke slightly disrespectfully of both your uncle the Admiral and your brother-in-law Dr Grant. But that showed good judgement on your part. Dr Grant *was* a selfish idle *bon vivant* and you were perfectly justified in disliking his imperfect treatment of his very amenable wife, your beloved sister. As for the Admiral, again it shows your own warmth of heart and loyal feelings that you resented the failings you observed in him as a husband to your dear aunt, and that when he introduced a mistress under his roof, you fled. Your morality can hardly be in question, and really the worst that Edmund could accuse you of is calling the adultery of Maria and Henry *folly* instead of suffering those sick shudderings of horror which afflicted Fanny when she heard of it. Edmund can be a little tiresome in that way, and you did try to bring him round with your saucy smile, but unfortunately on that occasion it only made things worse.

The warmth of your heart and loyalty to all those you love is evident in all your close relationships, with your brother and sister and aunt, but most commendably in your growing friendship with Fanny. You befriended and defended her when nobody else did, not in order to make yourself agreeable to Edmund, but because you felt genuine sympathy and pity for someone whom almost everybody else overlooked. Considering that Fanny never showed much gratitude towards you, I think that is evidence of real goodness on your part. You warned Henry not to hurt her by flirting lightly with her, and then, when he had fallen seriously in love with her, you were genuinely delighted for them both. You have a generous spirit, which is more than can be said for Fanny, however correct her opinions may be.

You even have the merit of being loyal to your old friends, though the better taste you acquired at Mansfield has quite properly lessened them in your esteem – another sign of good judgement. You were rather astonished when you found yourself attracted in the first place by a younger son without worldly prospects, but it is to your credit that Edmund's probity appealed so deeply to you. Your attempts to make him change his mind about his profession were perhaps ill-judged, but you are not to be criticized too severely for trying. You were being true to yourself in staking your last like the woman of spirit that you are. But as it happens, I think your feelings for him were only deepened by his steadfastness on this important point. You would have lost respect for him had he given in to your rather unfocused persuasions. As with other very feminine women, you like a fundamentally strong man. It is one thing during the days of courtship to enjoy bending his sturdy spirit to yours, and to revel in the delicious proofs of your influence, but you would not have liked a husband who was easily led, by yourself or by anybody else. Although you were first inclined to deplore Sir Thomas's strict authority as the head of his household, in the end you had to admit to Fanny that he was, in fact, your model of a good husband.

Well, Mary, it was not to be, and you and Edmund never did teach the world what connubial happiness is. But I hope you find plenty of consolations in your life in London with your sister. Many women would envy your lifestyle. Now that Dr Grant is so conveniently out of the way, you two women can do what you like, especially as you have plenty of money between you. I imagine you in a very charming Georgian town house, going about in your own carriage – perhaps a very pretty landaulette.

There will be the additional pleasure sometimes of Henry's company, and for variety maybe he will escort you from time to time on holidays by the sea or in the country – although I know you are not fond of sea breezes, and you have never shown much interest in Norfolk. Too flat, perhaps.

If I were you, I would not be in too much of a hurry to let any of those dashing representatives or idle heirs apparent attracted by your beauty get their hands on your twenty thousand pounds. In fact, do you really need to be married at all? You are not cut out for housekeeping, and I can't see you wanting to endure childbirth too often. In that sense, perhaps you had a lucky escape even from Edmund. Clergymen always have large families.

What you truly need is some engrossing outlet for your abilities, which are very considerable. That was why you took to acting with such relish and such success. You liked to try your powers in something new. Your talents are for the light and lively, your interests are men and women. Edmund said you read character well. It is clear that you have in you the making of a good novelist. Having some serious work to turn to every day, creating your own imaginary world to delight your mind, will surely be the very best way to put Edmund out of your head.

And to get your own back on your author, perhaps, dear Mary.

# NOTES

1. *The Mirror of Graces*, 1811; reprinted R.L. Shep, 1997.

2. Byrde, Penelope, *Jane Austen Fashion*, Excellent Press, 1999.

3. Austen-Leigh, James Edward, *A Memoir of Jane Austen*, 1870; reprinted OUP, 2002.

4. In conversation with the author, February 2016.

5. Austen, Henry, 'Biographical Notice of the Author', with *Northanger Abbey* and *Persuasion*, John Murray, 1818; reprinted with James Edward Austen-Leigh, *A Memoir of Jane Austen*, OUP, 2008

6. Bryson, Bill, *A Short History of Private Life*, Doubleday, 2011.

7. The series was accompanied by the book: Vickery, Amanda, *Behind Closed Doors: At Home in Georgian England*, Yale, 2009.

8. Austen, Caroline, *My Aunt Jane Austen*, The Jane Austen Society, 1991; also reprinted with Austen-Leigh, 2002.

9. Lane, Maggie, *Jane Austen and Food*, Hambledon, 1999; also ebook Endeavour Press, 2014.

10. *Jane Austen's Letters*, Collected and Edited by R.W. Chapman, Second Edition, OUP, 1979; *Jane Austen's Letters*, Collected and Edited by Deirdre Le Faye, Fourth Edition, OUP, 2011.

11. Austen, Caroline, 1991.

12. 'Cassandra Austen's Note of the Date of Composition of her Sister's Novels', private possession, reproduced in R.A. Chapman, *The Works of Jane Austen, Volume VI, Minor Works*, OUP, 1965.

13. Advertised on a playbill for the Theatre Royal, Bath in February 1795 as a musical entertainment. Tom Bertram refers to it as an afterpiece, which it originally was, but it proved so popular that it often became the main item on the bill. The farce was written by Prince Hoare in 1793.

# NOTES